Paddy Lightfoot was born in Potters Bar in Hertfordshire and at a very early age learned to play guitar and piano. On completion of National Service in 1957 he began a twenty-four year career as a professional musician touring much of the world and playing with the likes of Ray Charles, Count Basie, Liberace, and one of the creators of jazz, Louis Armstrong.

In the late nineties he settled in Norfolk where he co-authored 'Geoff Hamilton's Gardeners' Challenge' with his wife Marion, 'The Times Quis Challenge' with Robbie Somerset and 'The Quizzer' with Gyles Brandreth.

SIX MUSICIANS
AND A
BANJO PLAYER

Print

Subject:	Paddy L
From:	DAVID F
To:	terry@te
Date:	Sunday,

Hello Terry,

You may remembe
banjo with the
Anderson, clari

To get to the p
He used to phon

Having read his
<u>like to 'touch </u>
back so many ha

Have you got a

Sincerely,

DAVE FAWCETT

Paddy Lightfoot

SIX MUSICIANS
AND A BANJO PLAYER

REMINISCENCES AND RAMBLINGS
OF A TOURING MUSICIAN

Vanguard Press

VANGUARD PAPERBACK

© Copyright 2009
Paddy Lightfoot

A CIP catalogue record for this title is
available from the British Library.

ISBN 978 1 843865 75 9

Vanguard Press is an imprint of
Pegasus Elliot MacKenzie Publishers Ltd.
www.pegasuspublishers.com

First Published in 2009

Vanguard Press
Sheraton House Castle Park
Cambridge England

Printed & Bound in Great Britain

Marion-'Thank you for everything'

Contents

Introduction

By the end of the 1950s traditional or Dixieland jazz had established a growing following in mainland Britain due mainly to the musicianship and perseverance of a small number of enthusiastic and, in many cases, highly talented bands. It was an exciting time for British jazz bands and new outfits were springing up almost weekly as too were the clubs for them to play in. All the time the audience for the music was growing steadily. Steadily that is until the end of 1962, by which time I was a member of Kenny Ball's Jazzmen and something happened that, more than any other single event, helped to turn the jazz revival into a full blown jazz boom.

In November of that year the British Hit Parade took on a decidedly untypical appearance. Well, when I say untypical, Elvis was typically at number one but the number two spot was occupied by a recording of an old Russian folk song called *Midnight in Moscow* by the aforementioned Kenny Ball's Jazzmen, while in third place was Somerset jazz clarinettist, Acker Bilk, with his own composition for a children's television serial called *Stranger on the Shore*.

The success of these and other recordings had a positive knock-on effect on the popularity of jazz bands all over the country and soon vast audiences from the hitherto slightly reticent record buying public were flocking to fill clubs and small concert halls to hear the music.

It's against this backdrop that I set out the following random selection of reminiscences, ranging from whimsy to downright silliness, for your perusal. It was a fun time and if you were there and can still remember, I'm sure you'll agree. But don't worry if you are either too young or too far into your second childhood to be certain whether you were there or not. Just get comfortable, pour yourself a glass of wine, open the book and start reading. I hope it makes you smile.

It may make it easier for you to know that the band's line up for most of the sixties was as follows:

Kenny Ball – trumpet and vocals

Dave Jones – clarinet   John Bennett – trombone
Ron Weatherburn – piano   Ron Bowden – drums
Vic Pitt – double bass   Paddy Lightfoot – banjo
                               and vocals

Bill Bowyer – road manager

Waltzing Matilda

Besides being the key that unlocked the door to the more prestigious and more profitable venues in this country, the popularity of our own *Midnight in Moscow* and Acker's *Stranger on the Shore* soon became a world-wide phenomenon and provided both bands with the necessary credentials to take our music to audiences in places as diverse as America, Japan, Australia and the Eastern Bloc.

One big advantage of our international excursions was that we got a chance to hear the sort of jazz that was being played around the globe and our first trip to Australia introduced us to the music and musicians of a fine band led by the veteran pianist, Graeme Bell and almost instantly a bond of camaraderie and mutual respect was established, each band for the other. The fact that both bands were a mix of exuberant youth and mature experience meant that a love of jazz was not the only thing the two outfits had in common and we soon began to look forward to the all too infrequent occasions on which our bands would share a concert. Out clarinettist, Dave Jones, established a trend when he said at one such event, if a little grudgingly, "That band's pretty good for a bunch of wombats." Henceforth it was tacitly agreed that, when speaking of or to members of Graeme's band, we were to refer to them only as marsupials and not by name. Any creature with a pouch was permissible and all were in frequent use with the exception of 'platypus' simply because nobody was sure whether the plural was 'platypuses' or 'platipi'. We were soon brought down to earth when, after no time at all, we became known only as 'the pommie pop stars' and never Kenny Ball's Jazzmen.

It wasn't long before individual friendships developed between various members of each group so we were knocked out to hear, just prior to our third visit down under, that the bands were to share the first concert in Sydney and in celebration Graeme's lads would be at the airport to meet us with what was described as 'a musical welcome'. We heard on arrival that the gig had sold out well in advance so we were all a bit baffled, as we grabbed our luggage and passed through to the lounge area, as to why such a publicity grabbing welcome was deemed necessary. So imagine our surprise when, instead of a roaring version of *Tiger Rag* or *Muskrat Ramble*, the boys gave a wonderful 'a cappella' vocal rendering of *Waltzing Matilda*. It was simultaneously amusing and a little touching, performed with fine musicality and strong harmonies and was greeted at the end by genuine applause, not just from us but also the small group of world-weary, hard-bitten reporters and photographers who had turned out. Several uninvolved passers-by looked bemused, scratched their heads and adopted that all too familiar expression we'd long come to recognise suggesting that... 'no good will come from all this jungle music, you mark my words'.

This, then sees the start of an 'A cappella episode'.

The Sydney concert went a storm and the next day we moved off to New Zealand for a tour of concert halls and cinemas hauling up on day three at Hamilton on the North Island. After the show we were chatting on the coach back to the hotel as to how we would pass the time between now and going to bed. Now, I've heard it said more than a few times that as a result of the mental concentration involved in performing music and in particular jazz, because of the spontaneity involved, when it comes to things other than music professional players can be a little non-committal and laid-back at times and far from the glass being half full or half empty would opt for it holding just the right amount and I have to say my thoughts would be pretty non-committal. As if to prove the truth in this assumption, there was little conviction behind either of the two arguments for a game of cards or just a quiet drink or two to wind down. The tale from here on in demonstrates once and for all the existence of this jazz 'laissez faire...' Or does it?

That night, Ken, our leader, went for a business supper with the promoter who also happened to be the owner of the hotel we were staying in and pianist, Ron W, was doing his own thing, whatever that might be. As the coach pulled up to the front of the small, colonial-style hotel, which it should be said, had no

16

guests other than ourselves, we were as one man overcome by feelings of gloom and despondency to see the whole place in darkness. "Guaranteed what the night porter's gonna say," bemoaned Dave woefully. "It's more than my job's worth to open up the bar once it's been locked." Sure enough the figure that greeted us as the front door swung open displayed all the characteristics of the archetypal night porter, he was grey, thin, bent and old but his words could not have been less typical or more reassuring.

"Evening, gents, come in, the boss told me to see to it that you had a drink or two on him before bed and to be sure and have one myself." If he noticed, he never questioned the looks of relief and the near hysterical laughter that greeted his welcome, simply adding, "This way, gents," in a voice and accent worryingly reminiscent of a leprechaun on speed. After a brief powwow we decided that he should be referred to henceforth as 'AJ' standing for anti-jobsworth since the response we got having asked his real name sounded remarkably like 'Porridge'.

We followed him eagerly into the lounge-cum-reception area which was comfortably though sparsely furnished mainly with Lloyd Loom chairs and low glass-topped tables plus, tucked away in a corner behind a large palm tree, a baby grand piano. I say baby grand but going by the state of its yellowed teeth and dry, flaky skin, its baby-hood was some years passed. Waiting for the drinks I was sat on the piano stool doodling with a few chords when Dave approached looking something of a cross between sheepish and defiant, if such a look is in fact possible, and said to no one in particular. "That thing the wallabies did with *Waltzing Matilda*, you know that sort of barber shop thing? That was pretty good, wasn't it?" Assorted animal grunts and reluctant nods from around the room. "Mind you," he continued, "we could do it ten times better, us being a real band and them only Aussies." A sense of curiosity, almost enthusiasm was building in the room as AJ appeared with the drinks. "Cheers," said Dave. "We'll have another round while you're up, and be sure and have one yourself." We sensed the onset of an interesting and thirsty episode.

It was decided there and then that we were to be a vocal quintet with me taking the melody above a four part harmony from Dave, Vic, John and Bill, drummer, Ron B, having already established himself in a particularly comfortable looking Lloyd Loom, sipped his pint, lit a cigar and dealt a hand of solitaire.

Our personal 'Hallelujah Chorus' was to be a hit from our childhood by a group called the Four Aces with the non Handelian title of *Mr Sandman Bring Me A Dream*. It was a simple melody had some nice chords and really couldn't go wrong. We'd do the first eight bars tonight, knock off the rest on the bus over the next week or so and hit Australia with it on our return to Sydney. So, all we had to work on tonight was *Mr Sandman bring me a dream make her complexion like peaches and cream*, not exactly Cole Porter but so what? Ten minutes... tops.

Dave and John, our clarinettist and trombonist respectively, being typical jazzers enjoyed, if that's the word, only passing acquaintance with written music, or as John called it, "fly buttons on telephone wires", but in this case this was to prove a plus because whenever I did an arrangement for the band I would feed them their individual parts exactly as we were to do it that night. "Right," said John about five minutes later. "That's it; I reckon another round might be in order." By this stage we were feeling relaxed and smugly confident and were just beginning to enjoy ourselves when up came Bill. Bill was the band's road manager, who'd spent time working in the City and every evening before we left the hotel he could be seen in dark suit, dark tie, and white shirt with a detached starched collar rounding up stragglers like some immaculate border collie. Bill was one of nature's gentlemen and was always ready to help out so he was keen to join in the barber shop experiment. There is one more thing about Bill that I should perhaps mention. He hadn't a musical bone in his body. But what he lacked in musicality he more than made up for in stamina and about twenty minutes and two rounds of drinks later he was ready for a solo try out, or rather he thought he was.

Take my word for it. I was there. It was earth shatteringly painful and all Bill could offer by way of an explanation was, "I'm sorry, men, but I'm just having a bit of trouble hitting the first note."

The voice of wisdom came from the card table. "Hitting the first note? You couldn't hit a cow's arse with a banjo." Just one of Ron's sage and all-encompassing sayings that, though unarguably true, made absolutely no sense at all. Even so everyone knew its meaning.

"I think I know the problem," concluded Bill, looking decidedly shamefaced. "I need some lubrication. AJ, one more time if you please, and be sure to have one yourself."

Finally Vic, the band's double bassist, stepped up and thanks to a good musical ear and several pints of beer, was done and dusted in no time. All at once the room seemed to be full of people standing, sitting, or in Dave's case, lying with their fingers in their ears trying to hum their own parts to the exclusion of all others. I'd witnessed just this scene before at talent night at a Scottish folk club. Not something you can easily expunge from your memory. Worryingly, at this point they drifted towards the piano like a thick black London smog. It would seem we were ready.

I feel it only right at this point; however, to pause awhile and to challenge you to take a little gamble and ask yourself this question. Will an agglomeration of around sixty years of learning, practising, rehearsing and performing music stand these five would-be harmony singers in good stead, or will seven or eight pints of strong Aussie beer each take its toll on the audio faculties, the cerebral sensitivities and the innate musicality of these brave but possibly feckless pioneers as they undertake this hugely daunting but eminently do-able challenge?

So, back to the fray. A final clearing of the throat, a final humming of the opening note, a final swig of lubricant and from Dave, one final moment of defiant pride. "Right. Let's show those bloody dingoes what real harmony singing's all about."

One very final comment from the font of all knowledge. "You can't call them dingoes. Dingoes don't have pouches."

"Well, they bloody well will have if I get hold of them," said Dave.

The absurdity if not the enormity of the statement brought a black silence and then. One... Two...Three... Four... *Mr Sandman*... It was like a pair of dinosaurs in crashing, violent battle. It was like someone dragging a fingernail down a blackboard. It was like a pack of stray dogs being castrated without the use of anaesthetic. What it was not like, not even vaguely, was any form of music hitherto known to humankind. Dave took a drag on his cigarette on the count of three and was still coughing ten minutes later. John, for some unfathomable reason known only to him, believed it humanly possible to sing and drink beer simultaneously with predictably damp results for the rest of us. Vic sang *Mr Sandman* but in totally the wrong key, and Bill. Well, Bill, for reasons too dangerous to probe too deeply, gave a note perfect rendition of *She'll Be Coming Round The Mountain When She Comes*. Amidst all this mayhem I played all the right notes though, as Eric Morecambe might say, "not necessarily in the right order", and slid silently and painlessly under the piano.

A silence redolent of shock and awe before that phrase took on a more sinister meaning filled the room. On every ashen, terrified face were expressions of bewilderment and disbelief coupled with a brief but almost tangible hatred of all Australian musicians. The unspoken question on every trembling, querulous lip was, "What went wrong?" Well, no ifs, no buts, no if only, no excuses at all. In truth the shameful and shaming fact was that everything went wrong.

Dave speaking almost normally again broke the silence with a cough and faces, gaunt and haggard with disbelief and foreboding turned towards him. He spluttered, "Blimey, Pad, you gave us some bum notes to sing there, didn't you?" Although by now I had scrambled into an almost vertical position, weak and unsteady I was still determined to throttle him but before I could reach him Ron spoke.

"I thought you'd have this thing off to a tee in ten minutes, tops."

"That's it," stormed Dave. "They're not getting away with this. Come on, round the piano, we'll take it right from the start again."

Two or three were still too dumbstruck to utter a sound but Vic was able to voice their views eloquently enough. "Bollocks to that, let's have a game of cards."

Lloyd Looms were put at the table, sleeves were rolled up. Ron started dealing and John said in an accent more Iceland than Ireland, "Come on, AJ, stop snoring and let's have a drink here."

Four other voices added in perfect unison, "And be sure to have one yourself."

We played in silence for around ten or fifteen minutes before Ron confided, "You should have asked me before you started that racket. I had a chat with Graeme this evening and he said his lads have been doing that barber shop thing for about three years now. It's their main hobby."

All I could manage was straight to the point, "I'm not surprised, they're bloody good."

"That's as maybe," agreed Dave, "but it's a kick in the privates for anyone who says so in front of any of those wombats."

Stay Young and Beautiful

We stayed over three nights in Wellington to do a concert and a television show. To be in one place for more than one day was a luxury on tour giving us a chance to explore the town, maybe visit a local jazz club and to change our underwear. I probably mean launder rather than change. Although, then again in some cases, maybe not. On these particular three days I was sharing a room with John, our trombonist, in what was to prove an excellently run and pristinely clean family hotel. Now, clearly I have no idea as you read this, how old or of which gender you are but, whether or not you can still remember your own youth, I'm sure I don't have to point out that, as with most other twenty-something males, our bodies, far from being considered temples, were treated more like council rubbish tips with all sorts of junk food being poured into them each day, not to mention cigar smoke, the odd gallon or two of beer and countless heavy metals. We were all of us only too aware that this was not what we should have been doing if we wanted to still be playing at forty, so John and I decided there and then that we would quickly put a stop to the era of decline and abuse and revert to being the lithe, athletic Adonises we had been shortly after finishing our National Service only some five or six years ago. However, while you are no doubt still aghast at this manly but uncharacteristic decisiveness on our part I have to point out that we had taken this momentous pledge at least three times a year for, well let's say, some time. So, as Geppetto said when he finished carving his little wooden boy, "This is the real thing". But in the case of Pinocchio I'm sure I remember some reluctance when it came to telling the truth.

This then is 'The Legend of the Juice Machine'.

In preparation for our upcoming worldwide trip and the inevitable accompanying dedication to a regime of health and fitness, I had bought a book, hugely popular at the time, written by the splendidly named Gaylord Hauser, and entitled *Look Younger, Live Longer*. I recall at the time how succinctly that summarised our resolute intentions. Even if I were able to remember I wouldn't burden you or anyone, for that matter, with the exotic, outrageous and frankly sordid details of its contents and I'll only say that the key element in its biological sorcery was a combination of various health foods, and I use the adjective health against all my better instincts, to be consumed daily and for life, whichever proved to be the longer. In our quest for Peter Pan-dom we duly took our shopping list to the health food shop around the corner from the hotel and purchased, in bulk, packets of the following: molasses, honey, cider vinegar, brewer's yeast, and, to bind it all together in one glorious mélange, a hogshead or firkin or whatever is the measure for live yoghurt. Now, I'm sure you don't need me to tell you precisely where the ingestion of such a volatile, not to say explosive, concoction would be leading us socially. Or do I mean anti-socially? John and I, two likeable, thoughtful dedicated musicians became overnight outcasts, lepers, pariahs even, banned from approaching any gathering of normal human beings, forced to travel at the back of the coach with several windows open wide in all weathers. The fragrance (and I'm sure that's not how it was described by the aforementioned human beings) produced by the cocktail of interactive, while individually wildly toxic, substances was compared variously and unfavourably to that of rotting ostrich eggs, a decomposing badger and would you believe, even sewage works? We were accused, each and both, of being totally insensitive to the feelings of others of less robust gastric health, of hastening the end of our own pointless lives and, on more than one occasion, of 'crimes against humanity'. It was a while before we realised our cardinal error. It seemed that in order to avoid just such a malodorous catastrophe this super regenerative potion was intended to be consumed instead of our normal daily junkish diet, whereas we, in our headlong rush towards rejuvenation, had taken it simply as an additional supplement washed down by several pints of beer a night. Before we could be apprehended by the special NATO force hounding us on suspicion of creating a chemical weapon of mass destruction we decided to quit and to try and merge once again with the other less adventurous members of the band.

We returned a few days later to the shop where we had originally purchased what was described as the 'life changing' (how true) ingredients only to be teased by the very chummy manager, Ade, who would seem to have had some prior knowledge as to the likely outcome of our purchases even before we'd left his shop the first time around. We loosened up a bit at his Aussie sense of fun, although in our condition even a little loosening was almost too much. After a long chat he recommended yet another regime, this time one that he personally swore by and had adhered to for some years. Now I should say at this point that Ade was a god. Bronzed, Pan-like, vital and above all, cool. In fact all the things we wanted to be.

Apparently his youth and health promoting formula was a simple one and, if his own shape was anything to go by, a hugely successful one. We simply couldn't wait to get started. It seems that we were to juice several pounds of celery and carrots three times a day, pour it down our throats and watch the inevitable transformation. So, armed with one top of the range electric juice extractor (according to the mighty Ade only the most expensive was up to the task) and a small mule train's worth of the specified vegetables we headed excitedly back to our hotel room henceforth to be known as 'the lab'. We set up the machine on the night table between the two single beds and, after some minutes spent in prayerful homage, began juicing. To be honest and fair to Ade the concoction wasn't half bad so we were, as you can imagine, by now quite buoyed and determined to persevere. Three times a day we juiced our little hearts out and, out of respect for Mrs Turner, our hostess, duly deposited the carrot greenery and celery stalks in a neat little waste bin lined with a white plastic bag. Three times a day the bag disappeared along with its contents and was duly replaced by another. Now, for those of you who like to try and stay one jump ahead with these tales, I will give only one clue. From this moment on both John and I became objects of intense scrutiny by Mrs Turner. Several times I spotted her eyeing John with a quizzical and disapproving expression and he, likewise, reported the same furtive but baffled looks coming my way. Whatever her suspicions she was clearly never going to voice them. Not, that is, until it became time for us to move on. We'd packed our bags and loaded them in the coach and returned to the dining room for one last breakfast. It was obvious to everyone, not just John and me, that she had something to say and, finally unable to contain herself any longer the following conversation took place.

Mrs T:	"John, what have you done with it?"
John:	"Sorry?"
Mrs T:	"Where is it now?"
John:	"What do you mean?"
Mrs T:	"You know, the thing you and Paddy had in your room?"
John:	"I'm sorry; I'm still not with you."
Mrs T:	"Whatever you had in the bedroom. Where is it now?"

Suddenly the penny dropped. She meant the juicer. She'd taken umbrage because we'd been eating, or in this case drinking in the bedroom.

Paddy:	"Oh, I see. It's in my holdall. I've just thrown it on the coach."
Mrs T:	"What? It won't be able to breathe. It'll die."
Paddy:	"I can assure you it's already dead."
Mrs T:	"That poor little rabbit. You beasts have been feeding it for days, now you just suffocate it. You Brits can be so callous."

John and I looked at each other in disbelief as gradually the word formed simultaneously on our lips letter by letter.

R-A-B-B-I-T?

So there it was, the conclusion Mrs T had drawn as to the significance of the carrot heads and celery stalks had not been, as would have seemed to us pretty obvious, that John and I were doing our best via the ingestion of health-giving juices to salvage what was left of our decaying internal organs but rather that the stalks were the leftovers after a pet rabbit, or indeed even a whole family of the creatures had enjoyed a gourmet, death row meal or two on the delicious and indeed, juicy parts of the veg. Where, she had asked, had we kept it? A pivotal question if ever there was one, because any creature with even half an ear for music would, at the sound of John practising his trombone, have scampered squealing down the stairs with his tiny paws covering his offended ears. (I know. If its paws were over its ears it would have tumbled head first down the stairs, not scampered, but please humour me, it is, after all, only slightly less believable than the actual truth of the tale.)

Once we'd established that she believed that, rather than juicing the veg we'd been secretly feeding a pet rabbit, even at one stage a whole warren of them, the previously surreal conversation fell tidily into place. We explained our desire for some of what Ade at the health shop had and his assurance that, though it may not be the elixir of eternal youth, it had most certainly done much to give him exactly what we wanted. Or had it?

I could tell by the way she said, "He's a caution, that Ade," that their paths had clearly crossed before. "He's a lovely lad but I've spoken to him several times about his Brit baiting."

Undeterred, I said, "Well, it's just that it worked so well for him, it has to be worth a try."

"No," she replied. "I shouldn't think he's drunk a glass of juice in his life. No, that bugger could eat nothing but dingo shit and still look good. I mean to say he trains five hours a day as a member of the Aussie Olympic swimming squad."

We took it like men, how else, but as we climbed onto the coach I heard John muttering, "Brit baiting eh? I hope the bugger forgets to breathe in the two hundred metres freestyle and bursts."

But when the redoubtable Mrs T waved us off saying she'd have another word in Ade's ear we knew they'd both be falling about laughing at our expense at the Legend of the Juice Machine.

Football Crazy

I have heard it said of quite a few jazz players that when the time came for them to finally decide on a career they might have equally well chosen sportsmen as musicians. Mind you, the fact that they eventually chose a future of smoking (if not one thing then another), drinking (quite often to excess) and sleeping very little (mostly under an overcoat in the band wagon) must, I think, engender at the very least a spark of scepticism regarding their dedication to the sport ethic. We did eventually form a sort of peripatetic football team called, rather inventively I thought, 'The Jazzers' and there are one or two of our fixtures I shall forever have difficulty in forgetting. In the mid sixties we managed to squeeze into our exhausting schedule of non-stop training and exhibition matches a charity match, on their home ground, against a Stevenage Borough team (I'm fairly sure one of the charities was something to do with the care of injured and mentally scarred musicians). I myself played in goal, probably because two of the main requirements for a goalie are that he should be fearless and just a little crackers, strangely two traits vital in any would-be banjo player, and modelled my style on that of Pat 'The Cat' Jennings, a nickname he acquired because of his speed and agility between the posts for both Tottenham Hotspur and Ireland. Imagine, then, my disbelief and disappointment when even before kick-off I had attracted the soubriquet 'The Hippo'. To be perfectly frank we should have realised we'd made quite a serious misjudgement when, during the traditional kick in before the game, their players' shots were going either past or within catching distance of the goalkeeper whereas I, on the other hand, had no practice whatsoever since all the shots from our team went either well wide of the posts or several yards over the crossbar. Two or three going out of play not over the goal line but out for what would have been a throw-in had the match actually begun. But, save your pity, we were not downhearted for we knew that we had a few surprises up our sleeves. The right wing position had been allocated to Kenny 'Dasher' Ball who, though he had never actually played football before, remembered almost bumping into Sir Stanley Matthews on the beach at Blackpool and had agreed to turn out to help boost the amount of cash raised.

There being no limit to the man's bigheartedness, Ken had already made sure that we all at least looked the part by donating a very professional-looking strip consisting of long white shorts and black and white shirts, the vertical stripes being not only attractive in a peculiarly masculine way but also helping to disguise the fact that one of our more famous players had managed to acquire something of a portly figure or, as the reporter for the local paper put it, 'a very expensive beer belly'. Our leader's generosity could not, understandably, run to socks and shin pads and the two teams' relative familiarity with the game could be gauged by the fact that while the opposition were turned out in real football socks and proper foam and cane shin pads, our brave lads, on the other hand had to make do with two copies of that perennially popular but seldom read magazine, *Health and Efficiency,* stuffed down the front of the two longest socks we could find, matching or not. In my case, though, I considered it wisest to employ two copies of the aforementioned and pleasantly enlightening journal down each sock, the better to protect my less than robust legs. Legs, it must be said, that were generally acknowledged to be 'on loan from a seagull'. I don't know about you but, as far as I'm concerned, it seemed quite reasonable to assume that, since the event in which we were taking part was a football match, that the standard footwear would be football boots. See, you do agree with me on that. Well, we assume, you and I, too much. Monty Sunshine squeezed into the strongest footwear in his wardrobe, a pair of wooden clogs. Acker Bilk had to don carpet slippers to protect his in-growing toenail and Ken's decision to play on the wing in Wellington boots to avoid 'catching a chill', meant that during our pre-match kick about several of our players had to be stretchered off suffering quite severe head wounds inflicted by unidentified flying footwear. The opposite wing was left in the safe hands of Don Partridge, a one man band poised at number four in the charts with his recording of a song called *Rosie*.

A reluctant footballer, Don had only turned up after hearing that we were short of a 'winger for a charity gig' and mistakenly thought we were in fact looking for a 'singer for a charity gig'. The wing men's brief was simple, cunning and infallible. They were to hug their respective touchlines, wait for the pass and then simply pinpoint the big men in the middle. Okay, infallible may have been just a tad optimistic.

After twenty minutes or so we realised collectively that our strategy was possibly a little flawed since, every time the ball was passed out to the wingers, they were on the other side of the touchline signing autographs in the misguided and pitiful belief that the crowd were actually transported by their skill and speed on the field and needed a memento of this magic moment. Don at one point was to be seen in the depths of the crowd shaking hands and kissing babies in what I can only assume was his slightly underhand attempt to garner support and, more likely, sympathy from the Stevenage fans. We weren't too dismayed to go in at half time 2-0 down because we were confident in the knowledge that keen jazz fan and old friend, Derek Ibbotson, would arrive in time to start the second half. Derek was known the world over as an Olympic middle distance runner whose speed and fitness were legendary and who some years earlier had become recognised as the first runner in the world to complete a four minute mile. His impact on our dejected and, by now scarcely sober team was awaited with the highest of expectations and sure enough right from the start of the second half his speed was truly staggering as he criss-crossed the field, sped down the wing and popped up in the box. Oh dear, oh dear, oh dear. We should have delved a little deeper into the less publicised side of his sporting attributes, in particular his understanding of the basic tenets of 'the beautiful game', which turned out to be fundamental. No, let's be honest the phrase I'm looking for is, 'non-existent'. Throughout the forty-five minutes that he was on the field of play he made contact with the ball three times. Firstly, to take a throw-in, and let's be honest we should have had our suspicions right there and then as he insisted that it was, in fact, properly called a bully off. He next made contact with the ball or rather the ball made contact with him when a throw out from me struck him on the back of the head and caused enough concern for him to require prolonged treatment with the good old 'magic sponge' or as we called it, the brandy bottle. His final ball contact came when Ken had lined up the cross (he was briefly back on the pitch at this stage, by now clad in a sou'wester) for Derek who, to his credit, was perfectly placed to head home the winner when, in line with some bizarre rule of the game he had in his mind, he caught the ball, 'to see how heavy it was'. As he said later with masterly understatement, "It's not really my game." All in all we had a marvellous day and, thanks to the old world gallantry of the Stevenage lads, the final score was 2-2 and loads of money went to several good causes.

What I believe is called in the vernacular, a win-win situation all round.

Okay. Okay. Okay. No need to get so steamed up, you know, it's not good for you. I'm fairly sure I can put my finger on what's bugging you. It's been etched into our memory plates since the dark ages that the first man to break that physical and psychological barrier that was the four minute mile was the much vaunted and justifiably celebrated, Roger Bannister who, in May 1954 at the Iffley Road Stadium in Oxford completed the distance in 3 minutes 59.4 seconds. He was, as we all well know, assisted by the heroic pace-making of the two Christopher's, Chattaway and Brasher and his achievement is recorded and recognised around the world as being the first sub-four-minute mile. And, of course it was, but the key to this kerfuffle is that tiny but hugely important word, SUB. My earlier claim that Derek Ibbotson was the first man to complete a four minute mile is also true. In 1958 Derek ran a recorded mile in exactly four minutes and has been recognised ever since as the first man to run a four minute mile a fact dredged up for almost every pub quiz I've ever witnessed. Bannister's world-rocking achievement was to complete the distance in less than four minutes. I really do hope that my little ploy didn't get you too hot under the collar knowing, as I do that at a certain age that's not a good thing, but I'm sure you'll agree it's a great challenge for any dinner party or, dare I say, your next talk for the WI.

What we lacked in sporting ability we more than made up for with enthusiasm and only two weeks later we took to the pitch again, this time at Woolwich for a friendly against the local police or fire brigade, I really can't remember which, and in truth it is scarcely important. Either way they were fit and huge. Unfortunately, due to last minute gigs we were only able to muster nine players but the police stroke firemen were gentlemanly enough to lend us one of their eleven to make it ten a side. Our guest player was a chunky twenty-one stone right back who would fit in perfectly with our otherwise rock solid defence. Left back was the *Stranger on the Shore* himself, Mr Acker Bilk (who, it turned out was a total stranger to the game), his brother and manager, David, was centre half with our own John Bennett on the left. Right half was yet another clarinet ace, Monty 'Petite Fleur' Sunshine and the final line of defence was yours truly in goal. The previous weeks I had completely shaken off my offensive and frankly upsetting soubriquet with a dazzling display against an all-girls team from the world of classical music. I'll not try to disguise the unpleasant truth. It was a drubbing. We lost what had seemed to be an even game 7-1. I must say their first goal after about ten minutes caught us inexcusably unprepared. It was a free kick just outside the box and tore into the roof of the net faster than, or only slightly below, the speed of light. Unprepared I said and unprepared we were. Remember our left back, Acker? Well, he was at that time directly behind the goal trying to get his pipe to light in the breeze. Brother David, erstwhile centre half, was off the pitch right of goal savouring the home delights of a pint of Somerset cider while rugged and reliable John was putting on his overcoat because it had, as he said, "Turned a bit nippy." Surely though good old dependable Monty would be doing something useful. That depends how you look at it. Mr 'Petite Fleur' was ashen of face, trembling of leg bent over on the touchline being violently sick. So, I can see you have, in that annoying, cavalier way, decided we just weren't as dedicated as our opponents. Maybe, but that couldn't account for five out of the six remaining goals we conceded.

All five were, worryingly, own goals and all scored by a certain twenty-one stone fire stroke policeman, although in all fairness to him, he had meant them all as back passes. Now it's true that back in those innocent days before the discovery of metatarsals, soccer pundits or Wags, the goalkeeper was allowed to pick up or catch passes from any of his outfield teammates and the custom was to shout a short pre-arranged warning that the ball was on its way. In this particular case all five whistled past my head like a salvo of scud missiles, the sound of them smashing into the back of the net almost drowning out the whispered advice, "Your ball, keeper."

Still we enjoyed the fresh air and the celebratory pint or two afterwards and, as someone once said, "It's not the winning but the taking part that counts." What an absolute moron he must have been.

Glossary of Terms

I'm sorry but the Glossary of Terms does not signify the end of a very short book, rather it's a break with tradition in an attempt to smooth your journey.

It struck me when this book was nearing completion that a fairly large percentage of you may not necessarily be totally up to speed with some of the words or phrases pertaining to jazz in particular or, in fact, the 1960s in general or even, heaven help us, with music in any of its myriad forms. This, if it were so, must have made the first few pages more like a 'reading of the runes' than a refreshing ambulation along the esplanade of bygone times. So, well done you for being so persistent and resilient that you are still with us. So for those of you who were there but were seduced by the recordings of the likes of Presley, Richard (that's Little not Cliff) or the Beatles rather than the stuff trotted out by the threes Bs of British Jazz, Ball, Bilk and Barber, and for the other group among you who were, indeed, mesmerised by the complexities of jazz but who, by now have slipped too far down the greasy pole towards senility to even remember who was shot on the 22nd November 1963, let alone where you were when you heard the news. For all those deserving, discerning and delightful people I've compiled a short glossary of some of the more esoteric words. And I mean that in its dictionary definition of 'intelligible only to those with special knowledge', so don't start blaming yourself. I've held back until this point as something of a reward for making it through the preceding pages unaided. So let's have no more of this sulking and 'oh dearing'. It's all easy going from here on in.

Glossary of Terms

A CAPELLA

As or of the chapel. Now mainly used for singing with no musical accompaniment as in the barbershop quartets so popular at the beginning of the last century. They seemed to spring up as something to pass the time while waiting to be trimmed or shaved or whatever people did in barbershops in the nineteen hundreds. So, let's look at that again. From Monday to Friday the male population would sit thinking about it and discussing how best to do it. Come the weekend out they'd go and put it into practice. Certainly throws a little more light on the old phrase, 'Something for the weekend, Sir?'

AUSTRALIA

Not, as some of the younger people among you could be forgiven for thinking, the name of the aggressively arrogant cricket team who take such pleasure in 'sticking it to the Poms' but rather the country from which they come. On our band's first trip 'down under' as we jet-setting elite say, I was quite taken aback to discover that the entire population were not, in fact, ex-convicts with corks around the rims of their hats knocking back lager as though their lives depended on it. No, indeed, not by a long chalk. Around about ten percent of them were, in spite of the odd, half English language, little different from ourselves. Another surprise was to find out that Australia or, Oz as they quaintly and creatively call it, has produced some fine musical talent in the form of Dame 'Nellie' Melba, a world acclaimed soprano who had a dessert named after her (as in Peach Melba) and that equally famous soprano Dame Joan Sutherland who, sadly, didn't.

The country's claim to musical fame was not only in the operatic field either. The fine jazz pianist and bandleader Graeme Bell was also born there. Graeme should not be confused with Alexander Graham Bell who, though he invented the telephone, could not even master chopsticks on the piano. Yet another Australian-born musical colossus is Rolf Harris who having overcome the dreadful affliction of being born with an extra leg, went on to escape prosecution for tying down his kangaroo. Rolf achieved worldwide recognition for his virtuoso performances as a diggeriduist, dijeridooist... a wobble board player.

BAND WAGON

Not in this usage something upon which to jump because it is the thing to do but, in its more prosaic interpretation, a wagon to transport a band, not forgetting seven stage suits, and at least seven instruments including a double bass and a complete drum kit. So by the time you've squeezed in your amplifiers and sound system there's little room left for the band.

With increased success and popularity would come something along the lines of a small coach with driver and roadie but when I first joined the Kenny Ball Band transport consisted of a Volkswagen Kombi van with three front seats and a sofa and easy chair in the back with all the gear including drums and bass on the roof. Not too bad, I hear you say in that deprecating tone that is, I have to say, becoming a little too common. But I omitted to say that the rear seating though quite comfy was not secured to the floor in any way meaning that even the shortest trip felt like two hours on the dodgems.

Contrastingly The Ken Coyler Band toured the British Isles in a hearse, only deciding in a freak snow blizzard to ditch the coffin and bring the bass inside. Though I don't know for sure I would guess that a one-man band would fit nicely in a bubble car. With or without a roof rack.

BANJO

The banjo, although it is similar in shape to a frying pan, sounds incomparably better. What's that I hear? 'Not necessarily'. Just hold it there a second, you're starting to sound like a card-carrying, arm-band wearing member of the anti-banjo league. I have to concede that plaintive, haunting 'kerplunking' sound most often associated with the banjo may not compare too favourably with the sweet, sensual enchanting voice of, let's say, the viola or cello but to award it only second place in a two-horse race with a mere kitchen utensil that does not even class as a musical instrument and can only make any sound at all when whacked with a ruddy great ladle, is in my book, at least, beyond the pale and is a conviction that would, quite frankly, put a strain on the most rock solid of relationships. So, while it is fine for me to make derogatory remarks about the banjo I'd appreciate it if the rest of you would hold your peace for now.

The banjo's popularity was at its height in the early twentieth century when the Blacks and Creoles would use it as an accompaniment to the folk songs and work chants they would sing as they laboured hour after hour in the fields down in the delta regions of the Deep South. But it wasn't very long before they took their music further up the Thames to hamlets such as Gravesend and Thurrock and in no time at all violet sellers, barrel makers and blacksmiths all over the village of London were prancing around with gay abandon to the instrument's desensitising, robotic not to say hypnotic 'kerplunk'. Rather unfairly though someone plugged a guitar into an amplifier and the banjo player went the way of the juggler, the contortionist and the yodeller.

CLARINET

The clarinet is a single-reeded woodwind instrument. That means that the piece you put in your mouth, known incidentally, in that boring way that these Linnaean people have, as the mouthpiece, holds just one reed rather than two, as in the case of the oboe (an instrument not often encountered in the bordellos and jazz clubs of nineteenth century New Orleans). In the jazz fraternity it is often referred to as the liquorice stick because it looks not unlike... a stick of liquorice. May I draw your attention, at this point, to the hilarious, carefree humour and creative flare of the jazz world with regard to the process of naming or nicknaming instruments as opposed to the callous, not to say, sterile attempts of those in the classical field. Mouthpiece, that must have taken some time to come up with. Although when in play the clarinet is around eighteen to twenty inches in length it breaks down into typically four segments which fit into a case little bigger than a dictionary and weighing just a few pounds making it the instrument of choice for the more frail and sickly musician (or do I mean idle) who couldn't manage to manhandle a double bass, but who is not so frail and sickly as the pianist whose lack of vigour and general good health is matched only by his cunning, who manages somehow never to carry anything. A study of photographs of such clarinet greats as Benny Goodman, Acker Bilk and Monty Sunshine will reveal instantly that they are or were all, indeed, frail and sickly people (and probably idle too) although that's not always obvious from a photograph.

DENMARK

As a country Denmark is world famous for its production of bacon, blue cheese, sticky pastries and Hans Christian Anderson. So pretty well self-sufficient in the event of a global famine but Hans Christian puts them well and truly bottom, below Belgium, in the list of countries with the greatest number of famous achievers. In the mid-sixties the KBJB played a couple of outdoor concerts in the Tivoli Gardens in Copenhagen as had the Louis Armstrong band a few months earlier. The audiences at our gigs were typically Scandinavian in appearance and by that I mean they had long straight fair hair, slim, toned bodies, a few straggly bum fluff hairs on their chins and a foully aromatic pipe clenched resolutely between their teeth. Now you should know me by now but I'm going to resist the temptation to try and get a cheap snigger by saying something like... 'and they were just the girls'. In this case it wouldn't have been true anyway because that description was applicable to either gender. I'm not really certain just where or even whether I refer to Denmark in the text and in truth I don't much care whether I did or not I simply wanted a chance to acquaint you with your first 'Satchmoism'.

This is a salutary example clearly illustrating the danger of trying to use a foreign language without having first acquired a proper grammatical base. The problem here being that the speaker had not yet progressed beyond the present tense but was nevertheless happy to plunge in anyway. At Louis' concert a young Danish cub reporter had somehow attained an audience with the great man himself and, enquiring after the health of another of America's older jazz trumpeters, he asked, "Please to tell me, Mr Armstrong, sir. How is the health of 'Wingy Willis' at the moment?" The chagrin was evident on Louis' face as he replied, "I'm sorry to say 'Wingy' died last year." The reporter said, "I am indeed very sorry to hear this (and here's the problem). What is wrong with him?" Satch looked a little sad and finally replied, thoughtfully, "Well, I guess if you're dead pretty much everything's wrong with you."

By the way I've just remembered something else that would stand the Danish population in good stead on the global famine front. That is the loveable almost human creature, the Great Dane. I have to say that, while it is an unusually tall breed, it is very much on the lean side and would probably only just about feed a family of four for maybe three or four days.

DOUBLE BASS

The double bass is easily identifiable from its resemblance to a fairly mature tree with a man attached.

DRUMS

The jazz drum kit comprises a bass drum, a snare or side drum, a large and small tom-tom, a hi-hat and numerous cymbals of an astonishing variety of sizes. The drummer operates the hi-hat via a pedal with his left foot, the bass drum via a pedal with his right foot and the snare drum with mainly his left hand and the cymbals as well as other contraptions such as a cow bell, a wood block and a set of skulls with his right hand. All this he does simultaneously while grunting to himself in an untypically random rhythm. So. That certainly puts paid to the theory, some might say the boast, that only ladies can multi-task. Drummers are to a man wiry, taciturn, annoying and, above all... cool. I quote now a short story told to our own drummer, at the time Ron Bowden, by Mrs 'Mack', operator of digs for the entertainment profession. Mrs 'Mack' had a fairly large B&B in the Manchester area very popular with touring bands for two reasons. Her breakfast selection was unbeatable (if you were determined to commit suicide by cholesterol) and besides having three or four twin rooms, she could accommodate a further five in a dormitory out the back which, being reasonably quiet, was preferred by some of the more 'private' bands. It was in just this dormitory that a modern jazz quartet, no strangers to the delights of 'whacky baccy', was quartered. According to Ron, Mrs 'Mack' was reminiscing with stories of the jazz groups who had heaped praise upon her breakfasts particularly the slightly less than cordon bleu choice of fruit juice, cereals and 'the lot', a plate bearing just about everything from whichever country and from whichever animals that could be squeezed into a pan and fried. Her thoughts turned to the four modern jazzers of whom she had fond memories indeed. Not only did one or two of them manage two whole plates of 'the lot' but they were, she assured Ron, a nice close knit, caring group of lads. Ron quoted Mrs 'Mack' as saying, "You know, Ron, one evening I took them up a tray of tea to the dormitory, there they were all sat on the one bed passing their last cigarette from one to another. Isn't that nice? Although it did smell a bit odd."

DUFFLE COAT

Many years ago the duffle coat became the uniform of choice for a tranche of society consisting of weird people with frizzy hair, sandals and beards. Quite a number of men wore them too, as did many smart, discerning, elegant women about town. (My wife had one, say no more.) The coat itself was in appearance not unlike a large dog bed with the addition of a hood and was woven from a material similar to caramelised tapir droppings. My own investigations at the time convinced me that this was indeed the substance. Though shower-proof, the owner's manual suggested that it was unwise to get them too wet as they then emitted an invisible vapour with the distinctive odour of four-year-old wallaby urine and we all know what that's like. Their innate noxiousness and toxicity at this stage was surpassed only but that of another item of clothing favoured by the hippies, I'm sorry I mean, fashion conscious non-conformists, and this was the rather more upmarket Afghan Coat. Despite its permanent stench (this one, by the way, was fashioned from the soft underbelly of Norwegian goats with edging woven from their whiskers), it was accepted almost without question as being an essential part of the wardrobe of every classy, urbane female socialite of the sixties. (My wife had one of those, too.) But, back to the good old duffle. Its fixing system was quite revolutionary and flew openly in the face of centuries of dedicated research and development that had lead to the perfection of innovation and sheer 'je ne sais quoi' that is the button and, most suitably, the buttonhole. (I'll make no comment about the second language on the basis that, of itself, it trumpets erudition and charisma.) The duffle's alternative fastening arrangement of an oblong piece of wood being pushed through a loop of rope revived memories of the dark, desolate days of ignorance and superstition sandwiched between the Silver Age and the Tin Age. Yes, I speak, albeit in muted tones, of the Wood and Rope Age. This was in many ways a bleak time due mainly to the lack of any form of other solid material and those of you who have learned from my earlier texts will see at once why. Yes, of course. No metal equals no trumpets and no trombones, ergo, no... jazz. However, one man's meat is another man's poison (had you noticed... Latin, too?) and there was an upside to all this which was the popularity of the 'Banjomiterolophone' known, of course, to you and me as the Wood and Rope Banjo. Played throughout Norfolk and the South Western Cavern areas its study has provoked interminable polemics among musicologists and herbalists alike. It had, as you can imagine, a pleasant, soothing, if slightly ropeish sound and was used mainly as an accompaniment to the melodious but halitosic grunting of the squat and foul-smelling nomads who abounded in this era.

Favourites among their musical repertoire were such songs as *Wooden Heart* which you will recall was later revived with much success by Elvis Presley and *Norwegian Wood,* a lovely song later plagiarised by the Beatles. But first among all their airs and anthems, shanties and arias, top of their own particular charts and most requested piece on *Two Way Family Favourites.* Yes, you've got it. It was, of course, *Land of Rope and Glory.*

GIG

A term I've used repeatedly for fifty years or more without ever knowing its origin so I finally looked it up in the dictionary. It wasn't taxing to select the relevant meaning among the three given. Clearly, in our usage, it surely was not 'a two-wheeled one-horse carriage'; equally unlikely was 'a rowing boat or dinghy used mainly for racing'. No, it really had to be 'an engagement to play jazz etc, mainly for one night'. Even so I felt a little affronted by the all-inclusive use of the abbreviation 'etc', since the term gig was jealously protected from usurpers such as those from the classical world, as in 'we did a gig at the Albert Hall' for instance. (Although in our heyday Kenny Ball's Jazzmen did, in fact, play several times in that venerable chamber.) Others who would seek to filch the term for their own use were members of the sports fraternity, witness 'we're gigging against Spurs on Saturday at White Hart Lane'. Not the correct interpretation at all.

For reasons best known to herself my wife's mother, though corrected many times by me and others, insisted on pronouncing the word 'gig' as though it were spelt with a 'j' rather than a 'g', giving possibly the wrong impression to anyone inquiring after my whereabouts with the reply, 'I'm not sure but I think they've all gone jigging in Macclesfield for a few days'. Or even, 'No, Paddy won't be around for awhile, he's doing a jig at the Albert Hall'. For four and a half years her next door neighbour was convinced I was a professional dancer. If only she'd asked my wife. Marion's mum was, like a lot of people her age and generation, solidly opposed to change in any form and in her mind 'jig' was what we did and 'jig' it would remain. Now that

41

I've reached a similar age to that which she was then, I too am fiercely resistant to most forms of 'progress'. For instance, for me Mumbai will always be Bombay just a Sri Lanka is, and will forever remain, Ceylon. In my mind and vocabulary Beijing is still Peking and, of course, Iceland will always be referred to by its original name of Beejams.

The lady had, of course, every right to call what I did for a living 'jigging' (did I mention, by the way, that she was my mother-in-law?) as I have to continue to refer to Zimbabwe as Southern Rhodesia but I can't help feeling life could have been so much easier if a 'gig' had in this case been a horse and cart or a rowing boat.

GUITAR

John Williams wrote every single film score since the end of the First World War but didn't play the guitar. John Williams, on the other hand, played great guitar but was rubbish at film themes. Yes, of course. There are two equally well known musicians called John Williams. The first is an incredibly prolific composer while the other one is, along with such people as Andre Segovia and Julian Bream, one of the world's greatest classical guitar virtuosi. He was also for a short period of time one of my heroes at a time when guitars were still handcrafted and their tone and volume depended totally on the makers' skills. I said that he was briefly a hero of mine and the brevity of his influence was due to the fact that I quite soon discovered the jazz talents of the likes of Charlie Christian, Les Paul and, my all-time favourite, Barney Kessel. Barney (I use the Christian name in an underhand attempt to convey the fact that we were on very friendly terms when the unfortunate truth is that I never actually met him) along with the world's finest small-group bass player, Ray Brown, constituted two-thirds of the Oscar Peterson Trio. If you have never heard anything by this piano-led threesome I will only say, "Buy some and if you can possibly fault it I will publicly eat my Wellington boots." You may have to give me a couple of days notice to develop the taste as it's not something included in my Zen macrobiotic diet.

From this point in time it all went, well, if you'll pardon the expression, arse up. When an amalgamation of terrifying, uncontrolled electronics and a solid teak wall barometer became, despite massive objection from two or three folk musicians, recognised as a musical instrument. The birth of the electronic guitar was upon us. I'm sorry but from this point in history my mind is closed as regards the guitar except to point out that quite a number of people, particularly doctors and nurses, get confused and incapable of discerning between 'guitar' and the similarly sounding 'catarrh'. I must say I find this difficult to comprehend and, to be frank, a little annoying so pay attention while I explain. It's perfectly simple. One can produce a throbbing head, streaming nose, watering eyes and a painful pounding in the ears. The other is just a mild mucous infection.

IRELAND

This charming yet troubled island is steeped in myth and swaddled in folklore and superstition. The people are, as a rule, disingenuous and greatly influenced by and respectful of imaginary creatures called leprechauns. They are tiny little beings generally dressed in green who speak quickly and, on the whole, unintelligibly in a soft, lilting tongue evocative of peat, potatoes and porter. (By porter I mean Guinness but I just fancied a bit of allusive, allegorical alliteration. Would you believe it, two for the price of one?) Well, that's the Irish people. Now about the leprechauns. They are tiny little beings generally dressed… Well, you know all that, to be sure you do. (Whether that last language finally confirms my position as a polymath I'm not too sure but it must be a close run thing.) Affable they may be but the inhabitants are as a nation not the brightest sparks in the bonfire and there are, I'm told, two main theories as to precisely why this should be. Firstly, they spend much of their time dangling by their heels in order to kiss what, in all frankness, can only be described as a fairly grubby chunk of stone in the stalwart but totally ill-informed belief that they will somehow, as a result, become more normal, that is to say less green, taller, intelligible and so on, while actually the reverse is the case and they mostly end up greener, shorter etc. Their misplaced hopes are based on the theory that the inverted stance they are forced to adopt will drain more brain-nourishing blood from the seat of intellect in the feet. I must say there is absolutely no scientific basis for such aspirations so please do not try this at home. The other, more prosaic explanation for their less than normal knowhow is that they tend to spend every available minute consuming vast quantities of the thick black stuff called Guinness which leaves them in a permanent state of befuddlement and ensures the air of bemused, light-headedness so usually associated with people from this otherwise tranquil island.

The land itself is divided into the South, where the locals are compelled by statute to say the phrases, 'Begorah', 'not at all', and 'to be sure, now' at least eleven times each day, and the North or as we call it, Ulster. (Surely only the Irish would think of naming a piece of land after an overcoat?)

All this talk of islands reminds me that someone, so well known that I can't remember his name, once said or indeed wrote, 'No man is an island'. It goes on but that is the nub, the essence, the piece I want to pose a question about. It is this. Had the chap never heard of that large rocky outcrop in the Irish Sea just off the coast of Liverpool where the people are born with three legs, no tail and a passionate love of kippers? 'No Man is an island'. I'd say he may have to think again.

NATIONAL SERVICE

Until the early sixties every eighteen-year-old male with four limbs of roughly the right length and a pulse was invited to spend two years serving Queen and Country. After eight weeks of what was delicately titled 'square bashing', during which you learned how to drill, present arms, shave in cold water at five in the morning and, most importantly, polish the toe caps of your boots until you could see your face in them, you would be posted to protect our dominion from those nasty Russian chaps. Three rules for a successful National Service were as follows: Stay on the right side of the Motor Transport section since a lift into the nearest town or village on your days off was one of the only ways of staving off 'bullshit madness'. Cultivate as your friend someone in the admin block to be certain that that Holy Grail the forty-eight hour pass, did not 'get misplaced'. It was also imperative not to offend anyone employed at whatever level in the cookhouse. You'd be amazed at the range of insects or worse than can be concealed within a salad or the number and diversity of bodily fluids that can be stirred into a nice bowl of tomato soup.

There was, however, one stratum of authority to whom all of the above paid subservient homage and were, in return, treated with benign benevolence and it was to this saintly brotherhood that I pledged allegiance. Yes, you've got it in one. I became a lilywhite boy. A snowdrop. An RAF Policeman

NEW ZEALAND

An island situated in the Southern Hemisphere which, for those of you who flunked geography at the remand home, puts it even further south than the Isle of Wight.

The chief industry is sheep farming and a great number of the inhabitants rely on the humble sheep for many essentials such as food, clothing and in some cases even companionship and as in our own home colony, Wales, the manufacturers of men's Wellington boots do an unusually good trade particularly in the more remote areas. Visitors to these anachronistic and frankly fairly strange lands can expect to be confronted with the likes of hot springs, gurning Maoris, two or three fairly good mountain climbers and a frighteningly large number of Scottish emigrant ex-pats who, seeking the good life that is Australia, were, when it came to it, too drunk to get off the plane at Sydney.

Like the mother country, Oz, New Zealand boasts a vast and uniquely diverse musical culture called Kiri Te Kanawa who, like her mainland counterpart, 'Nellie Melba', also has a dessert named in her honour, and, no, I'm not going to tell you what it is. I think it's time you stopped milking the intellect of others and got back to working things out for yourselves.

The explorer and semi-pro banjo player, Abel Tasman, visited the islands in 1642 but the natives refused him entry because the silly old sausage had left his visa at home so he went off and discovered Tasmania, although, of course, he didn't know it was called Tasmania at the time. Now, that's what I call an amazing coincidence. What do you say?

Later, in 1769, Captain Cook explored the coastline and, on returning to Britain, set up his world renowned holiday company, Cook's Tours. Eventually the Maoris got to love the humorous and kindly British so much that, in 1840, they begged them to take over and colonise the islands, which from the kindness of their hearts they did. The rest, as the saying goes, is history.

PIANO

I realise it maybe a fairly foolhardy decision to take but I'm going to assume that even the least musically inclined of my faithful and erudite readers knows precisely what a piano is in either of its two main forms. One being the upright, presumably a reference to its... well, uprightness and the other being the grand, probably something to do with its relative grandeur or possibly the French for big. (Why the French should enjoy the kudos of having a style of piano named for them when I'm sure we're all agreed they're musically a fairly lacklustre nation I just don't know. I grant you Georges Bizet, Léo Delibes, Camille Saint-Saëns et al were proficient in a sort of Gallic way but, I ask you, Johnny Hallyday, Charles Aznavour? Let's be reasonable.) No, the two piano forms, should we all agree, be the upright piano and the big piano. But because, as I said, you are all, I'm sure, pretty well convinced of just what constitutes a piano I'll forego any further description and relay instead this sad and poignant tale charting the ups and downs of a fellow musician as told to me some forty-five years ago by our then clarinettist Dave Jones. It concerns an acquaintance of all the members of the band but who, for reasons of propriety and good old-fashioned gallantry, shall remain nameless. We all knew and liked him as a person but probably more so as a pianist, in particular his uncanny ability to play totally by ear virtually any song or musical piece new or old you might like to name. Like most of us he enjoyed a drink and whenever he was in his cups he became an uncontrollable and really unlucky gambler. It wasn't long before his reckless and selfish lifestyle had driven a wedge between him and his wife and children and eventually he moved out of the family home and into rented rooms. After only a few more weeks his craving had resulted in his being replaced in the band of which he'd been a stalwart member for more than seven years. However, determined to claw his way back to the limelight and the respect he had so enjoyed, he managed to get a job playing in a pub, mainly because of his innate ability to be able to accompany any song that the members of the public wanted to sing. A sort of karaoke night some decades before its time.

Dave told me how he visited, quite by accident, the pub in which the one-time great pianist worked and was amazed by the way he was able to pick up any song even those he hadn't heard before simply by calling on his years of experience and keenly attuned musical ear. Dave was, he said, saddened to notice just how defeated the man looked and just how shabby and world-weary both his physical appearance and his clothes had become. The pianist's garb was indeed tatty, ripped and stained almost all over with a particularly long split down the back of his trousers. In an attempt to preserve what was left of the musician's self-respect, but knowing that he would probably not even be recognised, he approached the battered upright and asked the man, "Say, mate, do you know your arse is hanging out of your trousers?" Without so much as a blink of the eye came the reply, "No, but you start singing. I'll pick it up as we go."

RHYTHM SECTION

This is the engine room of every jazz band providing the pulse and harmonic structure upon which the front line can weave its magic. Usually consisting of a combination of piano, drums, bass and banjo or guitar they paint an artistic canvas of subtle rhythmic nuances providing a syncopated polyphonic masterpiece to bring joy and fulfilment to audiences everywhere. Or, on a bad night they try their best to start and finish together.

ROAD MANAGER

Also known as 'roadie' or in the posh bands 'tour manager', they mostly drove the bandwagon, set up the gear on stage and generally shepherded and nursemaided (let's pretend that such a word exists even if it doesn't) the spoilt and generally mollycoddled members of the band. In my book there was only one such 'roadie' worthy of a mention and his name was Bill Bowyer and he was with the Kenny Ball Band for almost all the time that I was. Bill was a lovely man and a good, reliable mate but he was a little, how shall I say, un-streetwise. Bill wasn't even leafy lane-wise. Sharing the dressing room with members of Georgie Fame's Blue Flames at some university gig or another the Blue Flames tenor saxist asked Bill where we'd been playing lately. To which Bill replied, "We've just come back from a terrific tour of Romania." Which prompted the question, "Yeah. We've been offered a trip out there. What's the bread like?" Remember bread and honey = money. Bill, in all innocence, told him, "I can't remember exactly but it was a bit on the crusty side, but the rolls were okay." The rest of us present heard whatever street cred Bill may have had gurgling its way down the plughole.

The sax player, thinking it was Bill's joke, took it at face value and simply mumbled, "Cool man."

On another occasion Dave, our clarinet player, was getting changed, as were we all, for the start of the *Morecambe and Wise* television show which, just as a matter of interest, went out live (which with those two practical jokers around meant we were genuinely living on the edge). Dave was, as I said, in his underwear and had, for the first time in years, changed his pants. (Clearly I don't mean that the way it sounds. Dave, like the rest of us, changed his underwear at least three times a month, but what I meant was that, on this occasion, he was wearing a

48

different style.) His reply to Bill's enquiry was, "They're called boxer shorts," countered by, "Blimey, I'm not surprised they had a rebellion in China if that's what they were made to wear."

Great 'roadie' and genuinely nice man.

SAXOPHONE

A rich and diverse vein this since here we have a whole family of woodwind instruments invented by the Belgian, Adolf Sax (so you see Hercule Poirot is not the only Belgian to leave his mark for something other than making chocolate) in 1840 and patented six years later. The highest pitched of the family is the soprano sax which is similar to a straight, metal version of the clarinet but sounding rather like an agitated hornet justifiably annoyed at being trapped in a baked bean can. Probably the best known exponent of this, to my mind, least musical member of the group, is the virtuoso musician and composer, Sidney Bechet. Next lowest in pitch is the sweet little curved version called the alto saxophone most associated in jazz with the American maestro, Charlie 'Bird' Parker. However, on this side of the Atlantic, a fine player called Bruce Turner made quite a name for himself, at first as a member of Humphrey Lyttelton's Band and later fronting his own Jump Band. Bruce is credited with the introduction of the title 'Dad' to the British jazz scene, applied to absolutely everyone regardless of class, status, religion, gender or musical preference. (Before you go off the rails, I know and recognise that a good case could also be made for this accolade to be bestowed on either Acker Bilk or his erstwhile roadie Adge Cutler, either way it's the word itself that counts.) In what seemed at the time like a matter of hours the word had been assimilated into the vernacular of every jazzer in the United Kingdom as in 'Nice session, Dad', or 'What's yours, Dad'? Its whirlwind overnight popularity was due entirely to the fact that it did away with the daily drudgery of having to remember the name of the person you were talking to, or even playing with. A difficult enough task at the best of times but after a few 'sherbets', a bridge too far. An absolutely dreadful film was released, or should that be escaped, in the early sixties made only slightly watchable by the inclusion on screen of KB's Jazzmen. It was called, reflecting the era and with, I'm sure you'll agree, a hip, cool, crazy and cutting edge imagination, 'It's Trad Dad'.

But back to the sax family. The ubiquitous tenor has a sound not unlike a cormorant with a serious case of laryngitis but, nevertheless, became hugely popular with the exponents of swing and modern jazz. For what it's worth my own personal favourite stylists are Stan Getz and Lester Young but I'm sure you each have your own preferences.

The deepest and thus far the largest of the family is the baritone sax. Probably the one to which I am personally best disposed even though in the wrong hands it can, at times, be evocative of the fog horn on the Mersey Ferry. My liking for it is one hundred percent down to the sound produced on it by Gerry Mulligan who, along with trumpeter Chet Baker (later replaced by Bob Brookmeyer on valve trombone) fronted a pianoless rhythm section of just double bass and drums. Some of their tracks though, in particular, *Walking Shoes* and *Lullaby of the Leaves* would have, in my humble opinion, benefited greatly from the addition of a gently-strummed banjo. (Obviously you know me and my foibles by now and will realise, I hope, that I only put in the banjo bit for effect and that I didn't really mean it. Or, there again. Did I?) For the record there is, I'm told, such a thing as a bass saxophone although just how it sounds I simply can't say since the search is still on for someone strong enough and with powerful enough lungs to actually produce a sound on it. I could, if you like, offer a few possibilities. Like a hippo bursting through the sound barrier. Like the Rev Ian Paisley when he's really mad. Like a narwhal burping. But then why should I have all the fun? Give it a try, why don't you? It is a reference to the saxophone family that has given rise to what I am virtually certain must be the longest song title ever written. The title and lyrics relate, so I am told, to the leader of a big swing band trying to fill a vacancy in his sax section, but if you want my opinion, I reckon it's a newspaper wanted ad placed by a small town groupie after a one-night stand followed by a home pregnancy test. The choice is yours. The song, then, is called, and this time I really am in earnest, *I'm Looking for a Man Who*

Plays Alto and Baritone, Doubles on the Clarinet and Wears a Size Thirty-Seven Suit.

SIT-IN

Back in the late fifties William Wilberforce had only recently secured the abolition of the slave trade in Britain after a nineteen year struggle, but employment conditions were still contentious and sweatshops still flourished in the Enfield and Cockfosters areas as well as other hotbeds of discontent. The workhouses were overflowing and the poor and uneducated had no access to law and no one to champion their cause, Bono and Saint Bob being still many years in the future. The only recourse of the downtrodden masses was to withhold their labour in what became known as strikes. With the threats of closure of many of their work places the underclasses took to chaining themselves to their looms in what became known as 'sit-ins'. When Pitt the Younger was replaced in Parliament by Margaret Thatcher things changed for the better, Barry Manilow wrote some nice songs and strikes and sit-ins became things of the past. However, in this instance the phrase 'sit-in' has a totally different interpretation. Whenever jazz musicians had a night without a gig they would often take their wives or girlfriends for a night out on the town. Whatever lavish entertainment these dedicated family men might propose to their spouses, maybe a film premiere, dinner at the Café Royal or even a night up the local pub, were almost always rejected by the ladies who would insist on going to a jazz club to hear another band. Much against their own inclination the musicians would, of course, accede to the wishes of their loved ones and take them for a drink at the Blue Posts followed by an hour or so listening to jazz down in the nearby 100 Club. After a chat and a few pints with the band in their break he would be urged by his wife to play with the band in the following set to show everyone present how brilliant he was or, alternatively, to reaffirm the belief of every single member of the audience that he was, in reality, rubbish.

This was known as sitting in. Nothing to do with occupying a place of work but everything to do with giving your wife a wonderful night out and reassuring her of your unquestionable and amazing talent.

SOUSAPHONE

You know how it is. You wait for ages for an instrument named after its inventor and then along come two at once. John Philip Sousa was an American composer and bandmaster who undertook to create an instrument similar in range to the tuba, that is to say a brass bass (Remember? Like a huge trumpet lying on its side) more easily portable for the marching band. After years of development and research he came up with an enormous serpent of an instrument with a bell only a little smaller than the average flying saucer. The 'more easily portable' bit was simply that the player could climb inside the massive ring of brass formed by the serpent and march bearing the whole weight of the contraption, probably not much short of a couple of hundredweight, on his left shoulder. Personally if I were a brass bass player in Mr John Philip 'March King' Sousa's United States Marine Band I'd have taken in a sick note every marching day. The other main drawback was that its huge wide open bell became the nesting place of choice for the Lesser Black Backed Gull with the result that any of the band's seaside gigs would see the poor sousaphonist carrying not only the full weight of the instrument but in addition that of a life-size scarecrow strapped to the highest point of the bell. As if this were not sufficient in itself as a deterrent, the player would after eighteen months or two years of continual playing and incessant marching develop a massive muscle on his, or indeed, her left shoulder. Like the asymmetrical arms of the habitual trombone player, causing something of a problem finding a uniform to fit but, on the other hand, a pass to the very front of the queue at auditions for *The Hunchback of Notre Dame,* or Shakespeare's great comedy, *Richard III.*

TROMBONE

The trombone, along with the trumpet and clarinet already mentioned, constituted the front line of the majority of bands during the heyday of British jazz. It is pitched below both the other two instruments and its role is to provide the lower harmony and counterpoint. Right, that's the technicalities out of the way. Back in the old days in the Southern States of the USA, jazz bands were often employed to perform at funerals and in processions, frequently set up on an open-backed lorry. Unfortunately the slide of the trombone, which I'm sure you all know can move in or out about a couple of feet, would on occasion cause quite serious injury to whichever other member of the band was sat across on the other side of the vehicle. Teeth were cracked; eyes gouged out and, in one horrendous accident, a clarinet player had his instrument rammed almost halfway down his throat requiring urgent and complicated surgical procedure to retrieve it. (I do hope you're not chuckling at that possibility, this is the man's livelihood we're talking about. It does though, I must say, present, a strange picture, like some astounded heron trying to swallow a snake.) To ensure that the bands ended the parades with the same number of able-bodied players they had at the start an alternative was imperative. The only one which presented itself was for the trombone player to be sat at the rear of the lorry facing back down the street so that the slide moved out over the end of the vehicle. This practice, I'm reliably informed, gave rise to the name, still in use today, for a certain style of earthy playing called tailgate trombone. See, it isn't all just an excuse for a brief chuckle. Next time you're at a dinner party or an important company meeting or, indeed, anywhere where there are people prepared to be impressed you can trot out the origin of the phrase, 'tailgate trombone'. But there's even more. The action involved in playing the trombone successfully, and with as little risk to others around at the time, is to support the weight of the instrument with the left hand while at the same time ensuring that the mouthpiece remains in contact with the mouth at all times, while the right hand pumps the slide in and out. This, by the way, gives rise to the colloquial name for the instrument, the unappealing but apt soubriquet, 'slushpump'.

As a result of years pumping in and out all trombone players of more than six or seven years experience have one arm considerably longer than the other. Something of a nuisance when buying a new jacket but otherwise only really noticeable during a work-out on the parallel bars.

TRUMPET

If the contorted pipe that makes up the average concert trumpet were to be straightened out it would stretch for half a mile. In jazz the trumpet is musically the lead instrument.

Right. You've been caught red-handed. If you're having trouble concentrating take a short nap or better still swallow one of your tablets. Half a mile of piping must weigh tons and would need a whole bandful of trumpeters to even lift it let along keep it at the lips and blow down it. And in any case it would more than likely stretch to a few feet at most. I'll continue.

Virtually all jazz bands are or were led, that is to say the hiring and firing was done by, the trumpet player. The odd exception springs to mind such as Chris Barber, Max Collie and Charlie Galbraith who led on trombone. I seem to recall clarinet players, Acker Bilk, Monty Sunshine, Forrie Cairns and Sandy Brown who all fronted their own bands. George Webb the pianist and Mickey Ashman the bassist were both bandleaders in their own right, as were the drummers Eric Delaney and Lennie Hastings. There was, I have to say, even a banjo player who the rest of the Southern Jazz Band called boss. His name was Eric Silk. I repeat. Very few jazz bands were actually led in the 'pay the wages, take the bookings' sense of the word by trumpet players. I can say for certain, however, that all trumpeters without exception have moustaches. Just think of Harry James, Eddie Calvert and Kenny Ball. Even Joshua, he who legend has it 'fit de battle of Jericho' and who's playing caused the walls to come 'a tumblin' down' upheld that tradition and according to the 'good book', did 'wear a moustache on his upper lip much in the style of the Marx called Groucho'.

WALES

This is that big chunk of England that sticks out on the left hand side where the women all wear black traffic cones on their head and all the men are called, Dai. It was briefly an independent country separated from the Motherland by a huge ditch or, as they liked to call it, a dyke constructed by a chap called Offa. However, after the official Anschluss of 1951 it was filled in and the majority of the inhabitants fled to England and somewhere called Patagonia. Many sheep farmers still operate in traditional ways using antiquated machinery and practices, some even going so far as to castrate their llamas and alpacas using the ancient method of the noble but unsentimental Tuareg of North Africa. That is to say they simply bang a pair of house bricks together around the offending twosome and, bingo, it's all over. Recently just one such farmer was taken to court on the grounds of animal cruelty which he strongly denied. When asked by the judge, 'Surely, Mr Evans, castrating any animal in such a barbaric way must result in a great deal of unnecessary pain and suffering'? he offered the reply, 'No, your honour, your alright just so long as you make sure to keep your thumbs out of the way.'

The vast number of great jazz musicians born and bred in Wales is legend and includes... I'm sorry; I need some more time to think about that one. I can say for sure, though, that Britain's answer to Bessie Smith, the originator of blues singing as we know it is Welsh through and through. Unfortunately her name too escapes me at the moment.

So, having read and memorised the preceding Glossary you now have under your belt the necessary information to make your read a pleasant, amusing and educational one rather than something only slightly less difficult than deciphering the Rosetta Stone. It has, however, just struck me and probably you too that I have casually linked 'information' with 'under your belt'. Now, while both you and I know exactly what I mean it doesn't really make a great deal of sense, does it? 'Information', 'under your belt?' Personally I'd rate that as just about the last place I'd want it. A chicken biriani, steak and ale pie with chips or even four or five pints of bitter. Yes, no argument there. Under my belt, that's precisely where I'd like them to be but 'information' I'd see that as a bit of a no-no. Still, I've written it and we both know, you and I, just what I'm trying to convey so what the hell? I believe I'll just leave it. So, thus informed and fortified let's have no more of this tut-tutting and rolling upwards of the eyeballs, it really doesn't suit you. I can guarantee that

55

once you've got all the new information wherever in your body you'd best prefer it to be you'll understand the text henceforth as easily as skinning a cat. Well, there's yet another strange phrase. No? Sorry, just ignore me and read on and start enjoying yourself.

Have a Drink on Me

I've been asked more than a few times over the years just what
kind of people are jazz musicians and though I've given it quite
some thought I still have no better an answer than 'All types
really, but generally pretty nice'. These last three words may
well be the result of that well known softener of the jagged
edges of memory called the rose-coloured-glasses syndrome,
particularly since for me the sixties remain halcyon, blue
remembered days when television was black and white and
finished with God Save The Queen each night at closedown.
When London crime was kept uniquely under control not by the
police but by the Kray twins and Jack 'The Hat' McVitie and
when ladies of the night still walked freely through the streets of
Soho offering twenty minutes of sexual euphoria, hitherto only
the stuff of dreams, for just 'thirty bob and five bob for the maid',
which for those among you sadly too young to have experienced
those glorious, uncomplicated times but who have nevertheless
somehow managed to interpret these ramblings thus far,
translates into Newspeak as, 'one pound fifty and twenty-five
pence for the minder'. Indeed, although essentially a randomly
disparate group, jazz players are almost inseparably united by
the one great all-embracing passion and though the emotions
engendered one for the other may vary from a mutual respect
and admiration to a mere professional tolerance, even where
personal differences may have driven a wedge between two or
more musicians, a certain form of camaraderie will often still
exist nurtured by the recognition that each shares the same
unique talent. They are all capable of creating music
spontaneously from nothing. In fact so all-forgiving is this
ability to produce instant jazz, albeit of varying standards, that it
has been said that, had Herr Hitler himself been able to get to
grips with the wonder of Louis' trumpet solo on *West End Blues*
the recent history of the whole of Europe could have been

unrecognisably different with all of us jammin' in one huge Pan-European jazz band. All the same it must be said that all the vocals would most likely have been in German.

If you can think back that far you may well recall that this diatribe started as an attempt to provide a rational reason for the forbearance that exists between perpetrators of this... 'music of Satan' and there is another more probable and more mundane possibility. It is simply that all jazz venues with only a handful of exceptions were sited on licensed premises and, with equally few exceptions, all the jazz musicians I knew, regardless of age group, nationality and preferred jazz style, enjoyed shall we say the conviviality of a drink or two... or however many. So, now I believe we may be getting down to the nitty-gritty. Alcohol in excess, or rather the consumption of it has given rise to some pretty outrageous tales among musicians of all schools and probably only a small minority are totally true and unenhanced but one of my favourites involves the Mick Mulligan band of the late fifties and stars, if that's the right word, their trombonist, Frank Parr. I don't know about you but I find that these tales usually fall into one of three categories, (a) true and typical of the main character involved; (b) apocryphal, that is to say of doubtful authenticity and almost certainly embellished; or (c) total fantasy. It may help you to decide how best to pigeonhole this story for you know that I was told the first part in the Blue Posts, that's the muso's meeting place situated at the back of the 100 Club in Oxford Street, by Mick Mulligan and then the whole of it again by Frank himself at the same venue at a later date. It may, as I say, help you to decide its authenticity but, then again, probably not.

Frank Parr was born in Liverpool and was a keen and accomplished cricketer who at the age of twenty-five kept wicket not only for Lancashire but also the MCC. He played trombone with the Liverpool-based Merseysippi Jazz Band until 1956 when he joined the band led by trumpeter Mick Mulligan. He was a quietly spoken, convivial gentlemanly person of the old school and someone who I for one was always glad to bump into if I were out to hear some jazz and have a drink on a night off. His brash, no-nonsense style of trombone was well suited to the solid, unpretentious Dixieland approach of the band and their unconventional vocalist, George Melly. Frank, it must be said, liked a drink in much the same way that kids like Christmas or flowers like the rain and he was often to be seen leaving the aforementioned Blue Posts in a condition now often associated with showbiz or sporting celebrities who have drunk too deeply from the trough and described as 'tired and emotional'. But back in those open, honest, hearts on sleeves days we would just say legless.

The story of 'Frank's Folly' then goes something like this.

For some reason that doesn't turn out to be relevant to the meat of the tale, the band left particularly early for a gig at the Nottingham Jazz Club, situated rather perversely in an upstairs hall in West Bridgford. Having time to kill they stopped en route at a pub for what was, even by their own fairly expansive capacities, a long and overly liquid lunch. In spite of the extended stop they still arrived with plenty of time to spare and having set up the drums and uncased the other instruments they retired to the local hostelry, except that is for Frank who decided that the best treatment for his particular condition was to have a brief rest on one of the seats set out in four or five rows in front of the bandstand for the audience until he got his second wind. It wasn't long before his head dropped to his chest and he was snoring away like an old tractor struggling round a particularly muddy field. It is at this point I believe relevant, even essential to the story, to know the playing times involved at this and indeed most other clubs anywhere in the country at that time, so for those of you not fortunate enough (and I use the word fortunate rather against my better reason) to have visited Nottingham Jazz Club (or as it should be known, West Bridgford Jazz Club) in the late nineteen fifties here goes. All visiting bands played their first set of an hour from 8pm to 9pm and then, after a half hour interval, the final set from 9.30pm to 10.30pm. Back at the hall Frank had woken to find himself surrounded by the tittering members of the jazz-loving folk of Nottingham stroke West Bridgford and just in time to see the other members of the band setting up ready to play. Lurching zombie-like through the crowd he picked up his trombone saying to Mick, "Sorry about that, man, I nearly missed the first number." To which he received the curt reply, "What do you mean the first number? We're just back from the interval, you slept through the whole of the first set." Before Frank had time to absorb the enormity of this remark Mick tapped in *Riverboat Shuffle* and thus began Frank's gargantuan task of trying to keep the instrument to his lips while, at the same time, not pitching headlong into the front row of the audience. Most of the set seemed to have passed fairly uneventfully although the noise emanating from the trombone bore a striking resemblance to that made by a bumble bee trapped in a jam jar, and it has to be said in the titanic battle between man and trombone man came off a very, very poor second.

Eventually the band played the last number and to Frank the fact that it was not their usual closer and met with only polite applause caused only an ephemeral, moth-like buzz within his still-addled brain and he quickly packed away his instrument, staggered down the stairs and was soon in the band wagon and fast asleep.

Half an hour later at 9.30pm the remaining members of the band returned to the stand from the interval and played the second set. (a) True; (b) Apocryphal; (c) Fantasy? I leave it up to you.

British Jazz like Rock 'n' Roll, Beat, Punk, Garage, Carport and Lean To, after it, threw up its own fair share of non-conformists or, as we called them at the time, characters. Let's spend, if we may, just a little time looking at just a handful of them. Bob Wallis was a fine trumpeter and band leader whose singing voice could best be described as unusual. He was also an extremely nice man. Bob, unfortunately, had a glass eye and I'm reliably told that whenever the band took on a new member, on their first overnight stay when the band came down to breakfast the initiate would find an eye looking up at him from his fried egg. An experience guaranteed to either hasten the shaking off of the remains of a hangover or push the new man just one more step closer to dementia.

There is a tale of fellow banjoist, Dickie Bishop's determination that he should not lose two years of his life to National Service. It seems that, to this end, during his initial eight weeks square-bashing he would, as an indication of his less than robust mental condition, take every opportunity to walk down the railway line to London which ran almost through the camp. Picture it. "Squad dismissed." Off he'd go down the track. "This is your final warning, Bishop." Straight to the line towards London and home. On completion of 'jankers' he would stride off focused and determined to the track. Time after time the Redcaps would persuade him gently and considerately to rejoin the rest of his intake and time and again he'd head for London. If he ever got either home or demobbed on grounds of insanity, I never heard. Either way the experience did neither Dickie nor his banjo playing any lasting harm.

Clarinettist Acker Bilk had as his road manager for some time a fellow refugee from Somerset, who would keep the whole band in fits of genuine, tummy-wobbling buttock-clenching laughter from the moment the coach set off to the moment the last musician had been dropped off home. Finally, in 1976, he was persuaded that he should take this talent to entertain a little more seriously. His name? Adge Cutler and with the Wurzels he had a series of UK hit singles. Trumpeter and tubarist, if such a word exists, Rod Mason led a band called the Tamar Valley Jazz Band and his erstwhile drummer, Jimmy Garforth, told the tale of yet another banjo player who the band had taken on directly after a particularly alcoholic all-nighter, a decision almost immediately regretted. Too nice and too embarrassed to simply rescind the offer Rod opted instead to feed the newcomer misinformation regarding times, dates and venues in the hope that the penny would drop and the man would leave of his own accord. If it didn't work at least the band would get the opportunity to play mostly without him. The guilt and shame experienced can only be imagined as with about fifteen or twenty minutes left of the first gig remaining, almost in tears and demeaningly apologetic at having missed the job and let the band down he arrived saying, "I'm really sorry, man, I don't know what's wrong with me lately, I just keep getting confused. I think, maybe, I should see a doctor."

No more was said and I understand he remained with the band for some years to come.

Only recently a friend of mine of some twenty-five years standing pulled me up short in my tracks with this simple straightforward question. He asked, "Tell me, Paddy, how do you get the best sound from a banjo?"

In this particular case not such an everyday, run of the mill question as you might imagine. My friend, although he was aware of my pre-incarnation as a musician did not, I'm ninety-nine percent certain, know the difference between a banjo and a set of bagpipes. Of course, we, you and I that is, know only too well the nationally accepted truism that the main and unavoidable difference is that the banjo actually sounds like a musical instrument. Okay. When I say this is 'nationally accepted' I obviously mean by the genteel, civilised and musically informed people of the English nation living south of the border and not by those sad, lacklustre musically deprived folk further up. It would seem to me self-evident that Hadrian did not, why should he, build his wall to keep the banjoists in, after all why would they want to leave. No, the sole purpose of this tribute to the muse Erato was, patently, to ensure that the bagpipe players (if, indeed, players is the correct term for these musical assassins) to ensure, they kept their droning, barbaric, unmusical distance.

So, my friend's question again.

"How do you get the best possible sound from a banjo?"

All at once my mind was racing, delving back to those pre-war days when I was never without one. My reply was simple, to the point and untechnical.

"First you ensure your instrument is of a reputable make, a May Belle or a Vega would be fine. That it has a top quality vellum or plastic head. Fit a fine resonant bridge and finally equip it with the best set of strings you can buy. I think that about answers the question."

"Wrong," said my friend, to my mind a little too enthusiastically. "The way to get the best possible sound from a banjo is to throw it in a skip from thirty yards." He didn't laugh out loud, he's too well bred for that but I could see his shoulders shaking as he turned away, struggling to control his mirth and all too obviously guffawing like a drain inside.

Please, don't get me wrong. I am quite capable of accepting that the banjo, particularly in the wrong hands, does not produce the same soothing and mellifluous sound as, for instance, the lute or the harp and who in their right mind would disagree with that? It does have, however, a certain authoritative and, in the hands of a virtuoso, attention-grabbing 'kerplunk' to it which in my humble and unbiased opinion commands great and justified respect. (Who allowed this man to write this rubbish? Isn't there supposed to be someone in charge?)

You must agree, as sure as day follows night and May follows June, that nothing so mitigating could be said for my own particular 'bete noire' ...the tuba. Call me partisan, prejudiced, bigoted and unreasoning. I would not, indeed, could not, disagree. I just can't stand the tuba. Tuba players? Fine, the salt of the earth, dedicated, hard-working, conscientious citizens. Why else would they lug a hundredweight of metal around day in day out, uncomplaining? But the instrument no, I'm sorry, it just doesn't float my boat, light my fire, fire up the Quatro. (What a great series *Life on Mars* was.)

Over the years I have come across just three jazz tuba players (see, not that popular, is it?), all perfectly nice people. Bob Barclay was the leader of the Yorkshire Jazz Band, Rod Mason led the Tamar Valley Band and 'Squire' Gersh who, although he played double bass when touring this country with 'Kid' Ory, had spent some years with the memorably named Lu Watters Yerba Buena Jazz Band. (Clearly an informed, forward-looking, not to say cutting edge ensemble who had the wit, not to mention the bravery, to employ two banjoists, simultaneously.)

While I'm aware of hearing this yarn from one of these three, I can't for the life of me remember which one, so I'll just credit it to 'a tuba player'. I should make it clear right from the start that whichever band it relates to it was one in which there was no love lost between the man on the tuba and the banjo player. If the truth be known, they couldn't, for whatever reason, stand one another. So, let's have a little Vorsprung durch Technik about the tuba as an instrument. It looks a bit like a huge trumpet turned on its side and placed on the lap with its enormous bell pointing skywards. It's important that you commit to memory and retain the importance of this point. It seems that the player, along with all other of his ilk, had to defend against, as best he could, an eternal and down-grinding assault almost nightly. At clubs or dances when the alcoholic spirit had been summoned too frequently from his lamp and the combination of booze and bravado took its inevitable course, the cavernous, just-out-of-reach black hole that is the instrument's bell represented, to some in the crowd, a challenge too far. The gladiatorial sport would begin with scrunched up cigarette packets being lobbed towards or even into, and this was quite clearly the gold, the bull, the one hundred and eighty rolled into one, the bell of the instrument. A common occurrence as I say, and one taken in good heart by most bands. When later sometime down the path to alcoholic oblivion the game developed to include the slam-dunking of empty beer cans something had to be done. After much thought and hours of laboratory trials the answer became obvious and, on the very next gig, the tubarist in question unzipped his instrument from its cover to reveal a pair of ladies' tights stretched across the tempting, almost irresistible magnet, which was its bell. (Actually it appears his wife was somewhat thin of thigh so he joined together two or possibly even more pairs the better to repel the evening's anticipated missile attack.) All went well and the rest of the band were quite tolerant and good humoured about the fag packets now propelled in all directions as they trampolined off the top netting of the instrument. But almost inevitably things took a turn for the worse in the crepuscular hours as the projectiles became more sophisticated and their launch mechanisms more accurate. (I don't honestly know the stage of the evening it was but I do dearly love the word crepuscular.)

Suddenly from deep within the heaving mass on the dance floor an almost full beer bottle took to the air. It flew determined and raptorially like some predatory bird towards the bell of the tuba changing direction in the blink of an eye as it made contact with the protective barrier and flew, true as any archer's fletch towards the banjo player and, with a sickening crack, it broke his neck in two places.

Oh, come on. Stop that sobbing. I only phrased it that way in an effort to jolt you out of this apathetic torpor that seems to have gripped you lately. Of course the bottle broke the neck of the banjo not the banjoist.

The tale did, it seems, have something of a salutary outcome in that the poor, timorous, thunderstruck banjo player was so traumatised he never again felt sufficiently confident to take to the stage and the band played on for some years... banjoless.

A simple accident? Justified serendipity? Or some act too deep and dark to explore further?

In the early fifties I was playing the banjo fairly regularly at jazz clubs in the Home Counties and London with two bands at the same time and, since neither played more than one or, at most, two nights a week, it seemed to be working out quite well. Quite well, that is, until I took a phone call from a clarinettist in the New Orleans style called Cy Laurie. Cy was a well established professional band leader who, on three nights a week, ran his own jazz club in London's Windmill Street directly opposite the stage door of the world famous Windmill Theatre. The Windmill proudly advertised on its front façade WE NEVER CLOSED, a reference to their uninterrupted opening throughout even the worst months of the war when London was blitzed mercilessly by the German Luftwaffe. I was invited to join Cy's band and hastily agreed and was looking forward to my first gig as a pro at his club all the more eagerly since it offered the additional excitement of being an all-nighter. I was, at this time, still at school so it was fortunate that the session was to start on a Friday night. Imagine. Fourteen years old and playing an all-nighter in a jazz club in sleazy, unregulated, immoral London town. The kids in my class thought I was some sort of folk hero. My own enthusiasm, though, was slightly dented when I learned that of three bands booked for the graveyard shift, one o'clock to five in the morning, two were those with whom, for the next few days at least, I was morally obliged to appear.

Except for a four minute break during a piano feature, I played for seven and a half hours non-stop. Not exactly what I'd dreamed of as a career, but there was the consolation of earning in that night riches only ever imagined in my wildest fantasies.

As I mentioned earlier Cy operated one of the three most successful jazz clubs in London's West End at the time. The other two being The Humphrey Lyttelton Club at 100 Oxford

Street and Ken Colyer's in Newport Street just off the bottom of Charing Cross Road. The three clubs competed quite fiercely for customers with the employment of some serious, fairly aggressive publicity and the use of some of the best bands around at the time. It soon became all too clear that Cy's club was drawing more than the other two put together and it was only a matter of time before Cy, who was a deeply spiritual person and, in truth, very much a loner offstage, was being seen as some sort of religious oracle or fakir. Suggestions were even made that he had travelled in India and acquired some form of supernatural powers and, in truth, I have to say it was beginning to look that way. The other clubs were blaming poor weather for some equally poor attendances, but Cy's was thriving and I have to say that one would have thought a snow blizzard in Oxford Street must eventually slew southwest to take in Windmill Street as well. The other promoters claimed, on what grounds I'm not too sure, that he was able to employ a larger percentage of the top bands, and yet even with some amateur newcomers the only way to admit just one more fan would have been to peel off the wallpaper. It was finally agreed that it could only be the result of some greater, incomprehensible other-worldly power. Surely not. But let's examine the evidence. Three times each week the line of young mainly-male adolescents would stretch the length of Windmill Street and beyond, and as the doors opened one rolling, testosterone-fuelled wave would flood its way down the stone steps into the club below spreading wall to wall like the predatory march of hungry locusts, seemingly not even noticing the board announcing which band was playing that particular night.

At this stage I think it only fair to point out to those of you not intimately familiar with the West End theatres of the early 1950s that the Windmill was no ordinary venue. No *Annie Get Your Gun* or *An Inspector Calls* here. No, no, no. It was, in fact, the only theatre in London where the audience, consisting as it did, primarily of men clad, for whatever reason, in long raincoats, could stare totally unharassed for three, sometimes four performances a day at wholly naked female flesh. The overriding proviso being that the girls must, under no circumstances, move.

Now then, back to the line of spotty abnormally inquisitive youth. Obviously they couldn't wait for the opportunity to meet or even dance with one of these statuesque and, in their own minds, experienced women of the world, particularly if, as was likely, they'd spent much of the day staring at their nude forms on stage. Does it still need explaining? Okay, here goes.

Ever since the jazz club had opened Cy had issued free entry passes in perpetuity to all the female members of the cast. So the girls were able to keep a look out for rich husbands while the young bucks could dare to hope that one of these slightly flawed goddesses would, perhaps in passing, brush against their arm. So there it is.

Some sort of mystical, Rasputinesque sorcerer? I don't think so.

One very shrewd businessman? That's more like it.

I Guess I'll Get
the Papers and Go Home

So far as I'm aware no jazz musician joined a British band during the sixties, or at any other time for that matter, as the direct result of what I would describe as a formal audition. That is to say they didn't join the line of other hopefuls outside a local community centre or rehearsal room awaiting their opportunity to demonstrate their prowess by playing a couple of numbers to the accompaniment of a solo piano. Nor did their would-be employer sit halfway back from the stage invisible through the cigar smoke and general fug saying, between puffs, things like: "Okay once more from the top," and "Thank you we'll be in touch." These sophisticated scenes were just for films such as *The Glenn Miller Story* and *The Five Pennies*. But don't be too embarrassed to admit it if you somehow missed these classics from the golden years of La-La Land; they probably had less to say about jazz than did say, *Some Like It Hot*. I'm sorry but I'm just smiling to myself at the ending as Jack Lemmon, dressed and made up as a woman tells Joe E Brown that he can't marry him because he, Jack Lemmon, is really a man in drag, to which Joe E Brown replied, smiling, 'Nobody's perfect'.

But, back to the plot. Say that trombonist 'A' is less than happy with the way in which trumpeter 'B' is leading the Back Street Stompers and has decided, foolhardy, ill-informed and deluded though this decision is, he will quit the Stompers and form his own band. Simplicity itself. Well, not really but he has in this case no choice since his plan to quit is given greater impetus by the fact that he has put the band leader's sixteen-year-old daughter, how shall I put it? Up the spout and which fact will shortly be evident to anyone with even half reasonable eyesight. On nights off, which are few since the Stompers are a premiership band, he travels around the clubs in false beard and dark glasses listening to players he thinks would be good enough and sufficiently dissatisfied with their present lot to give a hearing to his offer of alternative employment. Being a keen traditionalist he needs to recruit five capable, non-violent and mentally stable chaps who'd be prepared to survive on slightly less than subsistence pay for the dubious privilege of joining his group. His line-up is to consist of trumpet, clarinet and himself on trombone for the front line and a rhythm section of drums, bass and banjo.

Having acquired his full complement of musicians his next step is to sell his car, re-mortgage his house and rent out his wife as a sex slave. Why, I hear you say, such draconian measures? Well, it's right about here that foolhardy, ill-informed and deluded come into play. His newly-formed band, no matter how good, can't earn a penny without stage suits, handout photos, a sound system and a bandwagon customised inside to include aeroplane seats and a rear bulkhead to store the gear. To add to his woes, in his enthusiasm to start earning he forgot to ensure that at least one of his group was teetotal meaning he must now find and employ a driver-cum-roadie to shepherd and protect his little flock. Not that the drink driving laws were quite as stringent back in those hazy, freewheeling days as they have since become given that the breathalyser was still some years in the future. So, as long as you were capable of hopping one-legged along a white line, whistling the theme to *Z Cars* while picking your nose without falling into the gutter, you were simply told to, 'Take it easy now, sir, and have a nice evening'. At which point you would be released to join once again the great mass of drivers sitting behind the wheel after having drunk what would today be around twice the legally acceptable amount of alcohol.

However, even before his new band has played a single club gig they have caused quite a commotion in the jazz world, since each of his men has left a vacancy in a premiership, or at the very least championship, group. Each of these positions has to be filled, more than likely from league one or, at a push, league two bands, causing yet more vacancies to be filled from… Where? The youth squad? Work experience lads? Street buskers? As I said quite a commotion.

Each move by any musician from one band to another would warrant a snippet in the *Melody Maker*, in those days quite a champion of the jazz movement. The piece would be along the lines that 'Trombonist 'A' has left the Back Street Stompers after four years to form his own band following musical differences with leader, trumpeter 'B'. He is to be replaced by trombonist 'C' from Charlie Brown's Dixielanders'. Just such a statement would appear at each resulting change. All very succinct and precise, However, I witnessed personally a dreadful aberration to this otherwise perfectly laudable system. Sitting in the Star restaurant in Old Compton Street one Friday lunchtime studying the aforementioned *Melody Maker* I was joined by an acquaintance of many years standing who was the piano player with one of the 'top bands' of the sixties and beyond. I'll veer away a little here to explain why the Star? Indeed that's a question I asked myself then on an almost-daily basis. Their spaghetti Bolognese was just about digestible if you were in the final throes of starvation, the tea was only slightly less toxic than paint stripper (this very same piano player with a 'top band' had returned a cup to the kitchen with the comment, "It would have been only humane to have shot that horse that did this."), and the coffee, well the coffee looked and coincidentally tasted not unlike creosote (although how anyone who knew what creosote tasted like could live to pass the knowledge on I find baffling) and its properties as a wood preserver were even more effective than the real thing. But, and it's a really big but, in their favour they had a vast cellar that ran the whole length of the building. So that in exchange for somewhere safe and dry to store drum kits, PA systems and on occasions a piano player too inebriated to get home even on public transport, in exchange for all that we were quite prepared to pay for the privilege of having our stomach lining protected against the ravages of whatever the British climate might produce in the form of wind, rain and sun.

So, there I was sitting, as I said, across from this pianist, reading through the *Melody Maker* when my eyes fell on a short paragraph in just the vein mentioned earlier saying that my luncheon companion had, in fact, recently given up his job with 'a top band' owing to musical differences between himself and the band's leader and had been replaced by a precocious young talent from the championship. When I asked him for the real reason he'd quit he grabbed the paper and began reading the piece. His expression slid from bemusement through hostility peaking at murderous hatred bringing me to what I felt must be the only possible conclusion. The snippet regarding his most recent career move was as much news to him as it was to me and was, clearly, not meant for publication till the following Friday.

He muttered almost inaudibly, "The bastard."

He yelled, causing the crockery to vibrate. "The bastard."

He bellowed, standing up, knocking over his chair, hurling the paper to the floor and leaping up and down on it. "The bastard. The bastard. The bastard."

Fortunately, for reasons previously stated, the six or seven other lunchers were all jazzers so to them this all seemed like normal restaurant behaviour although I have to say the three waiters cowered timorously in one corner.

I never did hear what happened to the over hasty sub-editor at the MM but what I do know for certain is that 'a top band' played that whole week without a piano player.

When Irish Eyes Are Smiling

In 1961 the Kenny Ball Band, of which I was by now a member, recorded as a single an instrumental version of an Old Russian folk song brought to our attention by Alan Freeman, our recording manager at Pye records. The song was, as mentioned earlier, *Midnight in Moscow*, and the fact that the treatment was purely instrumental was something of a gamble for us since up until then we'd had three top twenty successes but essentially as vocals. The arrangement was simple with plenty of top hat mules on the brass along with a gentle, danceable beat from the rhythm section which, added to the haunting, almost dreamlike quality of the melody, made for quite a commercial sound. Within weeks of its release *Midnight In Moscow* was vying for the number one spot with *Little Sister* by Elvis Presley, and a series of instrumental hits followed including *The Green Leaves of Summer*, *March of the Siamese Children* and *Sukiyaki*. Although Humph had registered a hit with a trumpet solo on *Bad Penny Blues* in the late fifties and Acker topped the charts with his clarinet and strings version of *Stranger on the Shore* not to mention clarinettist Monty Sunshine's poignant interpretation of the Sidney Bechet composition *Petit Fleur*, our version of *Midnight in Moscow* represented the first top ten hit by a full jazz band. Of course since then Louis had charted with his All Stars with *Hello Dolly,* but this was, like most of his hits, a vocal version.

On the back of *Moscow* Kenny Ball and His Jazzmen were soon in demand in countries all around the globe such as the USA, Australia, Japan, Romania and Fiji, but it is a tour much closer to home that sticks in my mind not least because it was quite simply a lot of fun.

Our first trip to the Republic of Ireland was quite an eye opener particularly with regard to the Irish Showbands, stories of whom we had heard from the two or three other groups who had ventured to the Emerald Isle. The showbands were a uniquely Irish phenomenon consisting usually of six to eight musicians and singers with, in many cases, quite prodigious musical talent who specialised (and this was their main attraction) in reproducing live on stage the top twenty or thirty singles at any given time as good as, and in many instances better than, the original recordings. It should maybe be pointed out here that in the late fifties and early sixties very few US acts made it to England and virtually none to Ireland, so that these all singing, all dancing, all playing groups were incredibly popular giving the Irish audiences a taste of what they were missing. One direct result of their immense drawing power was the appearance on the landscape of vast, hangar-like constructions in the very heart of the Irish countryside for them and, of course, any visiting UK bands sufficiently foolhardy or, more likely naïve, to play in. It should be said, though, that few acts with even fewer exceptions made more than one trip to this particular 'lion's den', one helping of humble pie being more than enough to take.

Their appeal and enduring popularity was such that some of the most successful among them enjoyed great wealth and power, in some cases even reversing the usual procedure by giving the promoter a small percentage of the door and pocketing the rest on quite a regular basis. So, it's not difficult to see why they would want to defend their turf so jealously. In addition the top two or three achieved great success in the states, but, and I've never heard a satisfactory explanation as to why, they made no impression whatsoever over here in Britain.

Well, as you might imagine, it was with some excitement and more than a little trepidation that we flew into Belfast airport and thence to the Grand Hotel. We arrived the day before our first gig and spent the evening drinking and chatting in the bar where we were eventually joined by our Irish coach driver cum tour manager, Nuggie McGrath. Nuggie was short, talkative, hyperactive and bore a remarkable resemblance to one of the elves in *Finian's Rainbow*. Don't worry if that particular musical is not among your favourites or, indeed, if you've never even heard of it. Suffice to say that Nuggie was... elfin. We could, incidentally never prise from him the origin of his nickname but surely no parent, however evil could, at the beginning of the twentieth century, in Ireland, or anywhere else for that matter, have so little regard for the future welfare and sanity of their baby son as to christen him Nugent. Nuggie, it must be said, coped well with this handicap and went on to tell us that all the jobs, a mixture of concerts and dances, were sold out in advance so it had all the makings of a nice, interesting tour. To best prepare us for the said tour, Nuggie, steering well clear of anything relating to the showbands, told us the following local allegory which, though I'd heard it a couple of times before, was so much better with the genuine Irish brogue.

The story concerns a tour undertaken in the mid fifties by Victor Silvester and His Ballroom Orchestra who were at the time a hugely successful radio and, in later years television, band. Victor specialised, as the band's name suggests, in playing strict tempo music for ballroom dance devotees and his adherence to the etiquette and propriety associated with the genre extended to both his and the band's on stage presentation in that Victor and each of his men wore immaculate evening dress finished off in Victor's case with black patent shoes, slicked back hair and a white buttonhole. The line-up of the group was fairly conventional with just two exceptions. The first of these was that they featured a violinist and an accordion player the better to interpret the very popular Latin dances and the second being that, unlike most of the bands touring in those days, they used no vocalists, the melody and the tempo being held as sacrosanct. Victor's music had, uniquely, a flowing, cascading almost dream-like quality to it achieved by yet one other variation from the norm and that was that the arrangements all included the sound of not one but two pianos set either side of the stage to form a visual and musical frame for the band. Indeed, so vital were they considered to the overall perfection of the music that Victor had it written into the contract wherever he played that two grand pianos in perfect condition must be at the venue and in place on stage before each performance.

Prior to Victor's first sell-out booking, which was co-incidentally at the venue at which we would also start our engagements the very next day, the promoter had search parties scouring the countryside and the surrounding towns and villages for two appropriate instruments and sure enough with only half

74

an hour to spare they both arrived, courtesy of two horses and carts, at the ballroom and were duly installed framing the stage from either side. So, near disaster avoided there, then. Not so I'm afraid. On arrival Victor took one look at the instruments and demanded an explanation from the hitherto proud promoter.

Victor: "These, as you can plainly see, are two UPRIGHT pianos even though our contact clearly states that you will provide two GRAND pianos. Explain please."

Promoter: "The contract does indeed say that we would supply two grand pianos and I can see why you might describe these two as being upright but I can say, without fear of contradiction that you'll not find two grander pianos this side of the border."

Alas, on each of the occasions I've been told this tale it has ended at this point so one is left to one's own creativity to append a final outcome.

Nuggie's narration received a rapturous and Guinness-fuelled reception after which plans were laid for the next day when he was to drive us just over the border into the Republic for our first encounter with a showband in the gigantic field of dreams that passed for a ballroom. We boarded the coach in the late afternoon intending to spend awhile at the venue running through a few tunes we'd recently added to our repertoire and after a very short drive arrived at the border crossing. Now, I feel I should point out that this was long before the escalation of the 'troubles' but there were, even so, one or two *Dad's Army* type skirmishes on a fairly regular basis, the commonest of these being the blowing up, or even burning down of the wooden sentry boxes that were used as control points on the more rural crossings, but no real harm was intended and the customs officer in charge of the post was always given plenty of notice in order to avoid any serious fallout between the two factions. So, no sign here as in later years of armoured personnel carriers, barbed wire protected lookout posts or British troop patrols, just a country lane in full spring blossom and a customs office. Well, I say office. There was, as mentioned earlier, a wooden sentry box equipped with a phone, a single hand-operated barrier across the lane and a cheery looking gent in a peaked cap with a clipboard. Nuggie greeted him as Sean Flynn and they chatted away for several minutes before Sean walked slowly up one side of the coach and down the other muttering to himself.

"A jazz band, eh? Well, there's a first." Stopping outside Nuggie's window he asked again. "Now then, Nuggie McGrath, what's that again you say you're taking over this fine spring day?"

"As I said before," replied Nuggie, "these gents are their Royal Highnesses, Kenny Ball and His Jazzmen."

"Jazzmen, is it? Well I hope you do better with them than you did with the load of cattle you brought across last week."

With that he tore off a chitty, passed it to Nuggie and wished us all, "Good luck to yer."

"And I might say good luck to you, Sean Flynn," replied Nuggie as he pulled slowly away, an elfish smile spreading slowly across his face. (No, I haven't left the 's' off selfish, it's meant to be elfish and if there isn't such a word then I've just created one.)

After only a matter of minutes we pulled in behind the enormous structure that later that evening would house some five or six hundred young people dancing, drinking and generally having a good time, but before we disembarked our driver stood up and turned to face us like a proper tour guide and announced, "Yer man, Sean Flynn, back there he didn't mean anything by it. It's just that when I'm not driving the bands around I'm in the lorry transporting whatever needs to cross the border, so yer see he meant nothing by it."

An uninteresting and unnecessary snippet but it did go at least some way towards explaining why wherever we went north or south of the border everyone seemed to know all about Nuggie McGrath.

After Nuggie and Bill, our own road manager, had put up our kit and shifted the piano into place we ran through a couple of numbers and then made our way to the dressing room through a huge archway not dissimilar to those used now for championship boxers to make their entrance to the ring for the big fight or maybe more aptly gladiators into the arena. A few minutes later the coach pulled up outside a nice little pub some two or three hundred yards from the border post and we were soon enjoying the first pint of the day. We'd decided to catch the last quarter of an hour of the showband's set to get a feel of the crowd and, in truth, to see what all the fuss was about. As the support band (a role they were not used to nor keen on playing) they had, unusually for them, opted to play just one long set to give them a chance to play all their hit parade tunes one after the other to finish their spot on the dot of ten thirty, after which there would be a half an hour interval with us closing the show from eleven to twelve thirty. So we pulled into the rear car park of the ballroom around ten fifteen and couldn't avoid the sheer drama of the scene that greeted us. There lined up side by side were a top of the range Mercedes coach and seven Mercedes estate cars. Quite a display and one which put things into perspective and also one which certainly could not have been lost on Ken, who was understandably proud of just having bought his first Merc on the back of the sales of *Midnight in Moscow*. So, there it was. The statement had been made, the rules of engagement posted and the gauntlet well and truly thrown down. We now understood the look of bafflement, even pity; on Nuggie's face as he listened to us rehearse. A look saying, he liked us and we were a nice bunch of lads but there was nothing he could do to prevent our impending sacrifice at the altar of the all-conquering showband. We were, you can imagine, all a little nervous and even Ken who was usually solid as a rock in this sort of situation seemed to be a bit edgy as he re-arranged our running order for the fourth or fifth time. A few minutes before we were to take the Lonsdale Belt walk onto the stage Ken and I were having a last minute brush up in the gents when the leader of the showband strolled in and the conversation went something like this.

Showband
Leader: "Good luck, lads, they're a terrific crowd, you'll not really go wrong. Just don't forget the Anthem."
Paddy: I don't think after all these years we're likely to forget to give them the 'Queen'."

SBL: "Oh, Jesus, if you play the Queen down here
              you'll not get out of the building alive. No, here
              it's the *Londonderry Air*... You'll know it as
              Danny Boy."
Ken: "Well, cheers, mate. I'm glad we got that sorted
              out."

Danny Boy was no problem since we'd put it out on an LP
the previous year, but to keep things simple Ken decided to do it
on solo trumpet with just some dirgey drum rolls behind. As we
grouped together at the top of the ramp down to the stage
Nuggie said, "Don't worry too much if they don't seem too keen,
they don't get much of the jazz over here. Just play the anthem
nicely and they'll forget about the rest of the evening, but
whatever you do don't mess it up or they'll crucify yers for sure."
And it was easy to see from the look of sheer horror on his
impish face that he felt sure that he would be found guilty by
association and that he meant, 'crucify' in the literal sense and
that he meant too, on the spot, where we stood, there and then.

After maybe three or four numbers our initial apprehension
(what I wanted to write there was 'our trouser staining terror')
gave way to relaxation as the crowd seemed to be on our side
and gradually we started to enjoy ourselves. A clarinet feature
from Dave Jones had some people at the front almost crushed to
death as the entire audience seemed to surge forward as they
applauded. Articles of ladies' personal and private clothing were
produced from out of handbags (at least I hope that's where they
came from) and were thrown at our drummer, Ron, some
hanging provocatively from his cymbals throughout the entire
set and each time John played a solo a group of local ladettes (a
word not in use then but still the best one) in front of him did
their own form of line dancing so explicit and so erotic they
would have been banned from just about every lap dancing club
around today on the grounds of gross indecency.

I can safely say with all due modesty and without fear of
contradiction that our final number brought the house down and,
having left the stage and returned a total of three times for
encores, Ken, deciding to quit while we were ahead, said
goodnight and signalled the anthem. It was at this point for no

logical reason at all that it struck me that Londonderry was a county in Northern Ireland and that the *Londonderry Air* must, to put it mildly, not be top of the charts in this part of the island. But, it didn't matter a hoot one way of another. Ken had his trumpet to his lips and we were all about to be torn limb from limb. Ron started an appropriately funereal roll on his snare along with a steady, muffled guillotine march beat on his bass drum. Our fate was sealed; the tricoteuses started their ominous clicking. All was lost but what came out from the trumpet could not by even the most tone deaf member of the audience be identified as the *Londonderry Air*. Instead the hall was filled by the most haunting, poignant and emotionally moving piece of music I have heard in a very long time, and as it reached its climax the people out front went totally berserk with unrestrained and generous delight. They clapped, they cheered, they stomped their feet, they whistled. Whatever Ken had played they loved it and later when the last of the still ecstatic fans had left the dressing room with handout photos and autographs we all focused our minds, as at the very best séances, on our leader eagerly awaiting an explanation. None was forthcoming until Bill put into words what we were all thinking and asked, "What in heaven's name was that lovely, lovely thing you played?"

"That I'll have you know," he began with mock solemnity, "was the Irish National Anthem. It's called *The Soldier's Song*."

"But I thought you'd settled for *Danny Boy*," said an even more puzzled Bill.

"No way. That lad was having us on, *Londonderry Air's* about as popular down here as *The Queen*. It's a bloody good job I came over here a couple of years ago with Syd Phillips and the first thing he did was to make sure we had *The Soldier's Song* note perfect and I'm bloody glad he did."

"What a bastard that guy was. I'd say he was after another scalp from the mainland," I spat out with genuine venom.

At this fairly electric point Nuggie seemed to have some information he was eager to pass on. "I looked out of the back door about twenty minutes ago just before you lads got off the stage and to be sure there was a whole convoy of Mercedes estate cars pulling out of the car park. I don't expect we'll see them in the pub for a nightcap."

So, cheered up, spruced up and buoyed up we walked into the little pub to a tremendous cheer from the customers and with a great effort and not a little regret we managed to turn down the majority of the pints offered without causing offence and eventually settled at a table with Sean Flynn, the customs man, and a few of his friends for a slightly less frantic drink or two along with an endless stream of amusing and relaxing blarney.

About twenty minutes and two pints later Nuggie and Bill arrived in the coach and were in turn besieged by almost everyone there for yet more handout pictures which Nuggie distributed to one and all using, in the main, their full names as in, "One for you, Pat O'Hara, you old devil and one for you, Con Logan, and one for the woman in your life. Oh, and here's one for your wife, too. That's for yourself, Mary Nolan, and don't go getting it all mucky now."

When the excitement had all died down after several more pints of the black stuff Nuggie tore himself away from his very own admiring fans and settled himself at our table.

"Well now, Kenny Ball and His Jazzmen," looking at no one in particular. "That went well. So it did. Next time you come by I should think you'll be offered the pick of the village virgins, all the free Guinness you can put away and twenty percent on yer fee."

"They did you better than the cattle after all, Nuggie McGrath," replied Sean.

"They did that," answered Nuggie. "But I was sorry, Sean Flynn, to hear that your little post was blown up again tonight."

"I think, as usual, Nuggie McGrath, you've been misinformed again, my little post, as you call it, is absolutely…"

BOOM.

"That'll be it now then," said Nuggie, matter-of-factly, sipping his drink.

Far Away Places With Strange Sounding Names

One of the least likely trips undertaken by the band took place in 1963 and took the form of a concert tour of Romania under the auspices of the country's National Arts Council. We were virtually unknown in the Eastern Bloc countries with the exception of East Germany, as it was then, where we'd established a circuit of concert venues over the past few years, so the reason behind the tour seemed to be shrouded in mystery. Our latest single, the by-now ubiquitous *Midnight in Moscow* had achieved some success behind the Iron Curtain so I suppose it's just possible that someone in the Arts Council thought we were some sort of British-based Russian folk group. To say that they were in for a shock was putting it mildly. We flew into the capital Bucharest, where we were to play our first gig the following evening and were picked up by coach and transported to the hotel where we met up with Sonia, our interpreter and Alexei our home ground tour manager. Sonia was an attractive, auburn-haired, outgoing woman of around forty. She was intelligent, inquisitive, spoke perfect English and hadn't the slightest idea who we were or what we did. This may well have gone some way to explaining her look of scarcely-concealed disbelief as she told us that all eleven concerts had been sold out for some time. So it had to be assumed that at least somebody had bought the record.

Alexei, by contrast, spoke not a word of English, a fact of which he seemed to be strangely proud, but then in all fairness our Romanian left just the tiniest bit to be desired. He was dark, thirty-ish and taciturn. So not a bundle of laughs there, then. Ken, our trumpeter and leader, hadn't been advised that a roadie would be provided and had brought along Bill, our own shepherd, mother hen, drinking companion and dedicated non-Romanian speaker. Thus, it slowly began to sink in that, unless we were very nice to Sonia, we were all about to spend the next couple of weeks unable to talk to anyone other than each other. It did mean, however, that with two roadies plus a coach driver Bill would be able to relax a bit and, not having to drive, might take, dare I say, the odd tincture or two. I can say with complete confidence that that's precisely what Bill thought too. That is until Alexei, having been introduced to Bill as the tour manager, decided unilaterally, otherwise, and left us virtually to our own devices. So Bill simply slotted in and carried on as at home, setting departure times, arranging pick-ups and generally nipping at our heels like some well-groomed sheep dog.

The concert in Bucharest the following day went a storm with just one slight fly in the ointment to which I shall return later.

The following morning we were to leave for the Black Sea resort of Constanza and as the result of some impressive co-ordination between Sonia and Bill, were settled in a non corridor carriage, gear stowed with the guard, all ready to go. Well, when I say all ready to go I mean all except silent, morose, resentful non-roadie Alexei, of whom there had been no sight since the concert finished, No sight, that is until the train was pulling chuggingly but unstoppably away from the station and he was spotted dashing along the platform like some sullen but deranged wildebeest sending luggage flying and leaping over other travellers. On closer observation I think that should read, leaping over luggage and sending… well either way he was a man in a hurry. As he drew up to the compartment, about six or seven down from the rear of the train, Bill opened the door slightly and reached out his hand, but just as Alexei prepared to make his leap his foot slipped and he stumbled leaving it up to Bill to grab at his coat and drag him bodily into the compartment. Puffing and heaving on the floor of the carriage he soon found his voice and launched into what was to us a meaningless non-stop babble till it dawned on him that we couldn't get a word of it, at which stage he spoke briefly to Sonia who in turn relayed the words, "Thank you, thank you, thank you, Bill." Then Alexei himself took up the mantra, "Thank you, thank you, thank you, Bill," eventually sinking into his seat and falling to sleep. From that moment it was blatantly obvious just how thankful he was as he worked like a Trojan, humping gear, struggling under vast piles of baggage and loading up the coach each morning, all the time repeating the only words of English he knew as though his life depended on it: "Thank you, thank you. Thank you, Bill."

Only three days later did Sonia, I believe much against her better judgment, reveal to us just precisely why.

Alexei it seems was married with three children, living in a comfortable state-owned apartment in Constanza. He also, however, had a mistress in Bucharest whose bed he was, judging from the debacle of the first day, very reluctant to leave. Sonia told us that, although she never managed to find out how, news of an earlier, but similar, dereliction of duty had made it's way to the ears of those who, in countries enjoying the iron rule of the Communist ideal, need to know such things and Alexei was carpeted and paroled to behave far more responsibly and to never, never lose contact with his charges for even a few minutes. Sonia went on to explain that for him to be caught out would spell total disaster for him and his whole family, resulting in the loss not only of his job but also his flat and, indeed, their physical removal, en masse, to somewhere offering, to put it mildly, considerably fewer comforts. Sonia made us promise not to reveal what had happened at the railway station to a soul and, since none of us were able to communicate with anyone but her, it seemed a fairly simple pledge to honour. Finally she leaned forward in her chair, by now trembling with what seemed to be a combination of emotion and apprehension and said, "I shall tell you one more thing at considerable risk to my own position." Slightly tearfully she continued, "Alexei is not and never has been a tour manager, or as you say, a roadie. He is, in fact, quite a high ranking member of the State Security Department whose responsibility is to ensure that you, all of you, see and hear only the good things of our country. He is also deep down a good and understanding human being." By now she had sparkling, icy tears on her cheek and looked at once angry, frustrated and above all, vulnerable. She smiled a gentle, grateful and quite childlike smile and added, "So you see his 'Thank you, Bill' is very much heartfelt and not simply as you say a parrot's phrase."

As regards Alexei the rest of the trip was fairly uneventful in so far as his role of escort cum warder became quite quickly an impossible one to fulfil since we had only to split into two or three groups after the performances to leave him in something of a dilemma. I also believe that he quickly realised that far from having any Bondian ideas or intentions we were just a bunch of simple souls who enjoyed playing jazz to anyone who would listen. On the day we left for the airport for the trip home Sonia was in tears, not I believe because she was going to miss us, because in all honesty being more used to travelling with youth orchestras and all-girl dance troupes, I'm sure we were more of a handful than she was used to. No, I just firmly believe that given the opportunity, she would have come with us. Alexei, looking a bit abashed and awkward as we each shook his hand and thanked him, finally turned to face us all and said, "I'd just like to say what a pleasure it has been to know you all and that under different circumstances and in different times we could have all become good friends. But that's the way of the world so, comrades, for now at least, farewell and have a good and a safe trip home." And, finally, still in perfect English, and without a hint of an accent he added a little thoughtfully, "You may be right; maybe I am at times as you say, a bit of a sullen bastard."

Before finally winding up this tale of our Romanian tour I'd like, if I may, to revisit what may well have seemed a throwaway line earlier in the text where I said something like 'the first concert in Bucharest went down a storm with just one slight fly in the ointment'.

It's a tale without a great deal of humour but it illustrates to my mind the diversity of responses and reactions from different people to the same situation. I should understand if any readers were to believe that the whole tale is trivial and uninteresting, even that I made the whole thing up just to fill some pages, and my reply to that line of thought would be simply, 'What's the point', this book had no preordained number of pages and is, as you would have had difficulty in not noticing, a fairly random recollection of anecdotes in no particular order and no set length. So, eyes down, brain engaged, here goes.

On our arrival in Bucharest the day before our first concert we noticed (it would have been impossible not to) as we were driven in from the airport that our trip had been heavily promoted with huge posters on buses, bridges and hoardings across the city. They were, of course, all totally incomprehensible to us except that they all featured a large action photo of the band along with a rundown, in English, of whom played what. That is to say, Vic Pitt-bass, John Bennett, trombone, Paddy Lightfoot-banjo and so forth. All, you would be forgiven for thinking, great publicity with ample info for the fans, and you would be almost correct. Unfortunately the blurb went on to say Ron Weatherburn-piano, Ron Bowden-drums and last but most certainly not least, I P Stanley-clarinet. Now I'm sure only a small handful of people remember, always supposing they knew in the first place, the clarinettist with Kenny Ball was at that time, and had been for several years, Dave Jones. This misprint or typo or whatever it was had us all laughing quite innocently including Dave who found the whole thing totally amusing. Mystifying, but amusing. We'll, I've just told an untruth because when I said that it had us all laughing I should have said, most of us, because Ken, our leader, seemed to take it all as some personal slight on Dave who, as I said earlier, didn't give two hoots and told Ken so. However, later at the hotel some fans produced some advanced concert programmes, in which, much to Ken's now escalating irritation, the same error occurred although by now Dave was answering to the sobriquet, I P. As mentioned previously we met up with out interpreter for the tour, Sonia, who brought with her a newspaper preview of the venues praising effusively the varying talents and accomplishments of each individual musician including quite a eulogy on the amazing technique of the band's long-standing clarinettist, I P Stanley. As a result early the following morning Sonia was dispatched to the headquarters of the National Arts Council, who had sponsored the trip, to see just what was going on and, more to the point, what if anything could be done to put it right. Meanwhile, the previous evening phrases such as 'What's yours, then I P?' and 'Give us a light, I P', had slipped too smoothly into the vernacular. Sonia's return bringing only bad news, the decision was taken to send in the heavy artillery in the form of ace problem solver, though it must be said, non-Romanian speaker, Bill, to try his luck. But, down in the mouth and with failure written all over his normally jolly face, he reported on his return that, although as in other equally intricate linguistic tight spots, he had spoken very slowly and particularly loudly and employed the maximum possible hand gestures, sadly no progress had been made. I don't know why but we all seemed genuinely surprised at this outcome. Bill had never failed before; it really was not going at all well.

Despite accepting that nothing more could be done at the moment Ken was palpably not satisfied that old chum and founder member of the band, Dave, had not been afforded the recognition he felt sure should be going his way and this unease stayed with him as we took the stage that night in front of the first of a run of sell-out audiences in the fabulous Bucharest City Hall. From the end of the first number it was obvious that the crowd, for so long deprived of anything Western, particularly in the field of entertainment, were determined to show their appreciation not only of the fact that we were performing on stage in communist Romania but also of the fact that they were enjoying, for whatever reason, the show we were putting on for them. Three or four numbers in it was time for the first feature spot of the evening and on this occasion it fell to me to vocalise on the old Clancy Hayes-Bob Scobey number *Ace in the Hole*. The crowd, though clearly understanding little or no English, clapped wildly at the mention of my name simply because it was among the half dozen or so lines in the programme in English and, at the end of the song whistled, hooted, stamped, cheered and generally enjoyed their own enjoyment. In order to quickly dispel any accusations of self-aggrandisement I should add that the reaction was the same for Ron W's rendition of Jelly Roll Morton's terrifying challenge, *Fingerbuster* and John's solo interpretation of *Avalon*. Only at the dramatic end of a version of the haunting Django Reinhardt composition *Nuages* from clarinet player Dave Jones, did the response flatten noticeably and although Dave, as usual, showed his mastery of his instrument and caught the delicate emotion of the piece as never before his reward was little more than a lukewarm round of applause without the earlier histrionics. This immediately seemed to rekindle Ken's annoyance over the whole I P Stanley fiasco.

We closed the first set to huge applause from an audience all too obviously having the time of their lives and in the dressing room Ken tried to hide his disappointment and edginess while Dave had a couple of beers and generally seemed to be totally at ease and content with the situation.

In the second half I sang a few more songs, some of them duets with Ken, to a rapturous reception. Ron and Vic's version of the Bob Haggart-Ray Bauduc classic bass and drum duet *Big Noise From Winnetka* came close to starting a riot of sheer delight as did Ken's own solo interpretation of *The St James Infirmary Blues*. Then with about a quarter of an hour or so to go Dave was featured on the old jazz standard *Chinaboy* to a muted and almost embarrassingly polite reception after which Ken, determined as ever, took the mike and said, "Let's hear it for the fine clarinet playing of our own Dave Jones." At which point the clapping simply petered out.

Having completed two encores we left the stand after a reprise of *Midnight in Moscow* and Sonia said it would be nice to get a round of applause for each of the guys individually, so Ken went back on stage and said something like, "I'd like to say thank you for being such a wonderful audience and ask you to show your appreciation for, on trombone, John Bennett. (John walked on to thunderous applause.) On double bass, Vic Pitt (even more noise, they were by now getting into their stride). On banjo and vocals, Paddy Lightfoot (one section of the crowd breaking into *Down By The Riverside* which I'd sung earlier. Strangely disconcerting in Romanian). Ron Bowden, our drummer and Ron Weatherburn on piano (met with the same wall of sound). And last, but by no means least, our clarinettist (a lengthy pause here)... I P Stanley." An explosion of noise followed, programmes were thrown in the air, seats banged up and down, feet were stamped in unison and, above all this two thousand delirious fans chanted... "I P... I P... IP... IP....IP..."

So, as they say, there you have it. I said at the beginning it wasn't a barrel of laughs, no hook, no punchline, no great denouement, but just what on earth was it all about?

The first publicity error was and still is, inexplicable. Ken's reaction understandable given that a member of the band had missed out on the recognition afforded the rest.

So why the bizarre response from the crowd? I can understand that the posters and programmes led them to expect

Kenny Ball and His Jazzmen and that this line-up included I P Stanley on clarinet so I can see their sulkiness at being foisted off with this stand-in, this parvenu, this Dave Jones person, but, for heaven's sake the picture in the programme showed the group with Dave included. And how, I wonder, did they imagine that Dave miraculously metamorphosed into I P Stanley at the very last moment? Or was it all presumed to be some devious Western ruse?

I don't know any of the answers and nor shall I ever, and certainly it's not of earth-shattering importance. I just happen to think it's worth laying out the variety of responses to one and the same set of events.

This tale of I P Stanley has set me thinking about the wider implications of why people should decide to replace their given names with a pair (or in some case, even a trio) of initials. For the sake of simplicity I intend, from now on, to call this the double initial syndrome. (I'm aware I just introduced the possibility of triple initials, but that's why 'sake of simplicity', so please bear with me as we negotiate this particular rocky outcrop.) The syndrome doesn't seem to suit just any old profession and is only really displayed to its finest in the cases of those with, shall I say, a literary bent. I can, for example, empathise wholly with the creator of that solid, imperturbable gentleman's gentleman, Jeeves, if after much paper screwing and pencil chewing he decided that perhaps after all Pelham Grenville Wodehouse was maybe the tiniest bit, well, front loaded and similarly would we, I wonder, be so irresistibly enthralled by those magnificent tales of Father Brown had the creator been, not as we know, G K Chesterton, but actually someone called Gilbert Keith?

The list of those who chose to fight life's battles with no proper first name is a lengthy one indeed but would we have been more comfortable or less so with Herbert George Wells, Alan Alexander Milne, or Thomas Stearns Eliot rather than the altogether snappier and intriguingly secretive H G, A A or T S?

As I think I said before the successful contraction seems to work with some aplomb in the field of writing but rather less well in other spheres, though I wonder whether the great Gloucestershire and English cricketer W G Grace would have been recognised as the epitome of sporting achievement at the cusp of the nineteenth and twentieth centuries as William Gilbert rather that the far simpler and even more majestic 'W G the legend'?

In the field of American jazz too the double initial is at a paucity save for the cornet player and composer of *St Louis Blues*, among others, W C Handy. Though he may have almost instantly regretted the decision when he realised just how puerile, not to say lavatorial, was the average sense of humour. In fact would he even still be remembered at all had he written under the more prosaic but less provocative titles of William Christopher Handy?

For some though the adoption of the syndrome was an outright necessity if only to avoid the blighted life and general ignominy that often accompanies a misplaced and tragic misnomer. I think mainly of that great Savoyard, W S Gilbert, and, having thought, doubt whether Arthur Sullivan would have formed so fruitful a partnership with him had he insisted on William Schwenk Gilbert. However, the trophy for the wisest application of the syndrome must go to the brilliant artist of *The Fighting Temeraire* and *Rain, Steam and Speed*, the incomparable J M W Turner, for opting not to burden us with the almost unmanageable Joseph Mallord William Turner.

Although, as I've said, not often hiding behind the mystery of a double initial – the members of the jazz fraternity were attracted by the cache and glamour of a nickname. Who could suggest that those two aristocrats of big band jazz, 'Count Basie' and 'Duke Ellington', would have made so great a mark as plain old 'Bill' and 'Ed', while John Birks Gillespie is most surely less evocative of a high note, be-bop trumpeter than 'Dizzy'. (If you thought the 'Count' and 'Duke' really were members of the nobility I'm sorry for shattering the illusion but I'm afraid we're all grown-ups now and eventually the truth will out.)

But, for my money by far the most impressive soubriquet originates in the bordello days of the Crescent City and belonged to one 'Jelly Roll Morton', pianist and leader of the band known as 'The Red Hot Peppers', (See. What goes around comes around.) his nickname meaning almost anything to do with the sex act you want it to was, nonetheless, only slightly more memorable than his given names of 'Ferdinand Joseph le Menthe'. But I know which I'd have answered to if, like him, I'd spent the early part of my career playing piano in the euphemistically titled 'sporting houses' of New Orleans.

All this talk of pseudonyms reminds me of a comment made by the great Louis Armstrong, whose nickname, Satchmo, incidentally is a contraction of Satchelmouth and refers to the unusual size and shape of his embouchure (the shape formed by the lips and face muscles in order to produce a sound from a brass instrument) on one of the occasions on which I met him. (You may well be thinking that my use of the phrase 'one of the occasions' is perhaps a device to try and convince you that he and I bumped into each other on an almost monthly basis, when in fact, I met him only twice, and you'd be right.) It was at the second of these meetings which took place (and I just love writing this) at the Savoy Hotel in London where the rest of the band and I had been invited to join the great man in celebrating his 68th birthday in 1968.

Also present were jazz promoters, jazz chroniclers and in general the great and the good of the British musical press. (I'm sorry that this is becoming a chapter of bracketed items but I'd just like to observe that the words 'great and good' and 'press' must surely represent that wonderfully named literary device, the oxymoron. No, not a dullard from one of our oldest universities but a figure of speech with conjunctions of apparent contradiction. If you knew that already then GTTTOTC.) So, there we were, as I said, at the Savoy Hotel, a small herd of us gathered around the great man in what was I have to say fairly banal conversation, when the question was posed. "How do you prefer your first name to be pronounced, Lewis or Louis?"

Louis' reply was simple, "I don't mind, it's Lewis or it's Louis, just so long as folks remember I'm Satchmo." Louis himself I might add, pronounced his name Lewis as in Lewis Hamilton the F1 racing driver rather than Louis as in Robert Louis Stevenson of *Treasure Island* fame.

While in the realm of Louis' quotes I feel I must let you in on an example of his simple but hugely appealing sense of humour. This episode took place on the occasion of our first meeting when the band was chosen to play support to Louis' All-

Stars for a short British tour. We'd finished the first half of a concert and two or three of us were taking up positions in the wings to witness the jazz legend in the flesh for the first time. The drummer and bassist of the All-Stars were there too waiting to take to the stage when Louis and his 'medical advisor' sauntered up and drummer, Danny Barcelona, asked, "How are you this evening, Pops?"

Louis' eyes glistened, his smile broadened. It was as though he'd been waiting all day for just that question. "Well, Danny," he replied, "Old Pops ain't so good. Doc here tells me my blood ain't far enough apart." Before we had a chance to analyse and absorb the horrific implications of such a devastating diagnosis, he continued, "Yeah, he says I've got very close veins."

We all chuckled more with relief than amusement while Louis almost fell over laughing and in between each bout of totally uncontrollable mirth he replied, "Very close veins, I got very close veins." Then he turned towards the stage, wiped his trumpet with his hanky and, still smiling said, "Okay. You All-Stars, let's make some music for these nice people."

And that's exactly what they did, and how!

I've often heard it said and have no reason whatsoever to doubt that as we get older our memory can become less reliable, less retentive, less analytical, even. That said I'm fairly sure that Romania and the name I P Stanley had some recent relevance to what I've been writing so I'll try and pick up the thread as best I can. The whole I P business has, on occasion, caused me to wonder whether the original error had repercussions elsewhere, perhaps in some parallel existence and, having wondered, I feel convinced that that must have been the case. So, picture the scene if you will.

In a smart London bookshop a proud and excited author is seated at a table, pen at the ready, preparing to sign the flyleaf of his first eagerly awaited novel for a whole bevy of bouffant and blue rinsed ladies queuing patiently in front of him. He permits himself to muse a little, recalling those awful garret and cornflake days spent struggling with this, his own magnum opus. But that was all in the past now and he'd even overcome the deplorable adversities that went with having been christened by uncaring and clearly heartless parents, Isador Perseus Stanley.

91

The transformation came after a few barren years spent in the wilderness of literary obscurity when the brainwave struck like well... a brainwave. After his abrupt awakening and his subsequent adoption of the double initial trick his talent was soon recognised and well rewarded and the double initials imbued him with a new importance, a new air of experience and above all, a sense of mystery. He rebuked himself silently for not making the discovery earlier for had it not been staring him in the face in bookshops all over the country? P D James, for example, was read in almost every country the world over, while, J K Rowling was a millionaire many times over. So now it was the turn of I P Stanley. He adjusted his spectacles as the first of his fans approached. He picked up his pen, she opened his book, he took it from her and laid it on the table. This, then, was what it had all been for. She leant forward and smiled coyly, saying, "Would you be so kind as to write 'Helen, I hope you enjoy the book. Yours, Dave Jones'."

The Morecambe and Wise TV show with, left to right, Ron W, Ron B, Paddy, Vic, Ken, Dave and John. Someone really should tell Ken his hair's on fire.

Vic in typical action man pose

Ron wonders what won the three fifteen at Newmarket

Paddy, Vic, Dave, Ken and Ron B, try to decipher the Enigma Code.

One trumpeter gives another trumpeter a silver disc.

KENNY BALL AND HIS JAZZMEN

The photographer has to be female and naked. Otherwise
why are we all so cheerful?

Dave Jones, Acker 'Stranger on the Shore' Bilk and Monty 'Petite Fleur' Sunshine all playing the clarinet except Acker who's lighting his pipe. Not forgetting vocalist, Beryl Bryden.

Born on the fourth of July. Louis' birthday luncheon.

Just one of the perks of being leader. You don't have to
wear your pyjamas at Tokyo airport.

Waiting for yet another plane. This is the only known
likeness of Bill Bowyer, roadie 'par excellence' fourth from the
left.

Pianist, Colin Bates and a banjo player in a straw hat on the run from the style police.

Brother Terry, trumpeter, Allan Elsdon and the ship's idiot.

Eventually we saved up enough and traded them all in for a
band wagon.

ITINERARY FOR AMERICA, AUSTRALIA, NEW ZEALAND, AND SINGAPORE

```
May   6th  - Charleston, W. Virginia
May   7th  - Grand Rapids
May   8th  - Jackson
May   9th  - Day Off
May  10th  - Day Off
May  11th  - San Antonio, Texas
May  12th  - Day Off
May  13th  - Day Off
May  14th  - Los Angeles
May  15th  - Day Off
May  16th  - Fly to Australia
May  17th  - Perth, Capitol Theatre
May  18th  - Adelaide, Thebarton Town Hall
May  19th  - Melbourne, Festival Hall
May  20th  - Canberra, Albert Hall
May  21st  - Brisbane, Festival Hall
May  22nd  - Sydney, Stadium
May  23rd  - Fly to New Zealand
May  24th  - Auckland
May  25th  - Auckland
May  26th  - Hamilton
May  27th  - Wellington
May  28th  - Wellington
May  29th  - Palmerston North
May  30th  - Day Off
May  31st  - Napier

June 1st   - Brisborne
June 2nd   - Dunedin
June 3rd   - Christchurch
June 4th   - Christchurch
June 5th   - Timaru
June 6th   - Day Off- Fly to Sing
June 7th   - Singapore
June 8th   - Singapore
June 9th   - Singapore
June10th   - Singapore
June11th   - Singapore
June12th   - Singapore
June13th   - Singapore
June 14th  - Possibly
```

Who said the bands work harderenowadays? A fairly typical
itinerary from the early sixties… And a banjo player.

The lads sitting on a park bench. Fortunately none of us ended up sleeping on one.

A Jazzers Eleven outing. Paddy 'The Hippo' takes control while Dave fiddles with his glasses and John heads of for a quick pint.

The front line can't actually play those instruments, they
just carry them for effect. Nice, aren't they?

High Society

I returned to the UK in September 1957 having completed what was then a mandatory two year period of National Service with the RAF in Germany spent mostly with a tiny signals unit just a few miles from the town of Münster. My life at this time was musically pretty bewildering in so much as I spread my copious spare time between playing piano in a typical German March-Waltz band while at the same time filling the piano stool with a modern jazz group a la George Shearing Quintet. As if this were not sufficiently confusing I also played guitar with a predictably efficient but sterile Teutonic Dixie band while broadcasting on BFN as vocalist-guitar strummer with The Blue Mountain Boys, a sort of country and skiffle group formed within the unit. So, on my de-mob I felt confident that I was pretty well prepared for what was going on in the UK music scene. Wrong. Wrong. Wrong. The charts were an absolute jumble of styles and stylists dominated largely by Guy Mitchell with *Singin' the Blues*, Elvis Presley with *All Shook Up* (he incidentally had an amazing fourteen singles in the top forty in just twelve months), Harry Belafonte and *Mary's Boy Child* and an old friend of mine, Lonnie Donegan with *Cumberland Gap*, number one for five weeks and *Puttin' on the Style* at the top for three. I'm sure you noticed, since that was the whole point, that I said Lonnie was an old friend and though we'd been out of touch for the past two years, during which time he had become a megastar, our relationship had, nevertheless, been in existence for several years. We first met at Wood Green Jazz club in the early fifties when he was the banjoist with the Chris Barber Band and I was doing the same job with the Phoenix Jazz Band, who on that particular night were filling the gaps between Chris' sets. Lonnie was older and, I have to say, better than I was and took on the cloak of a mentor since we both played a similar style of banjo. I'll digress here if I may because it has struck me at this very moment of writing that Lonnie may have quite a bit to answer for to those of us who opted to persevere with a career in jazz since, although that's precisely where Lonnie started, he went on and almost single-handedly created and popularised what became known as skiffle. (I know there were The Vipers, Dickie Bishop, Chas McDevitt and Nancy Whiskey and many more, but I did say 'almost single-handedly', so let's be realistic here.) As a result almost every guitarist in the hit groups of the sixties claimed that skiffle and Lonnie in particular were what made them take up the instrument, which in turn led to rock 'n' roll and we all know who won the contest between jazz and R & R in this country. I didn't really mean that as a serious polemic but it would make an interesting discussion subject at your next dinner party. Or then again, maybe not.

Lonnie and I continued to bump into each other on tour as we often shared the billing on concerts so I was glad some fourteen years after our Wood Green meeting that, when he was invited to record the 1966 World Cup Anthem, he chose Kenny's band to back him. Convinced that my services would not be required (Lonnie always played the banjo part on his records himself) I looked forward to a comfortable, relaxed day in the box. He had, however, different ideas saying that he would just do the vocal this time. When I asked why, he said, "Cos this is my session and, anyway I think you're about up to it now, you old sod." I didn't mind the 'sod' but thought the 'old' was a little strong. I was twenty-nine and he was thirty-five.

But, let's be honest when your friend and erstwhile mentor pays a compliment it's surely churlish to object at all so I just smiled, unlocked my banjo case and said, "Cheers, Lon."

The record we cut, *World Cup Willie,* went on to sell well. I went on to record, with Ken's band, a total of fourteen chart successes. Lonnie went on to put thirty-four singles into the British listings while his albums sold millions worldwide. Willie too had at least some influence. England went on to win the world cup.

But to return to 1957. It wasn't just on the music scene that you would have noticed some huge differences from today. There have been such astonishing changes in almost every walk of life that, at the moment of writing this down, I find almost too much to credit. For instance in those simple, simplistic days if you had an important message to convey by phone when you were not at home you happily joined the queue of patient, smiling people and good humouredly jingled your tanners and brass threepenny bits (I'm sorry about the possible, unpleasant picture that the use of the term 'threepenny bits' might conjure up for all of you fluent in cockney rhyming slang but there you are, threepenny bits I wrote and threepenny bits I meant) until it was at last your turn to enter the smoke-filled, pee-smelling solitary confinement cell that was the Public Telephone Box. Evil as they sometimes were they at least spared us the quite depressing sight and sound of whole railway carriages full of, presumably, adult humans with a flat piece of metal seemingly surgically grafted to the side of their face for the entire journey.

The ugly Orwellianness of the scene topped only by the ignominy of standing by the chiller cabinet in Waitrose while the zombie at your side yells 'Hello, Babe, I'm in the supermarket in front of the fridge and they ain't got no chicken legs. What shall I do?' God forbid Babe's man might have to beam back to earth, engage his brain and make a decision. (So you've guessed by now I'm not the biggest fan of the way personal communication is going.)

But, for now at least, back to boxes. I was always cheered and reassured by the sight of those lovely old AA boxes (no, not as you might think some form of roadside rehab). AA in this case standing for Automobile Association, beacon of hope and sanctuary for many a motorist back in the days when cars were manufactured with built-in obsolescence. The AA man would sit astride his motorbike and sidecar alongside the aforementioned box and was duty-bound to salute all cars bearing the AA badge. That's what they said, but we all knew it was us they were greeting. My favourite box, however, with its aura of security and protection was the big, blue Police Box and had we known then that they were all so much bigger inside than out and could so easily break free from the limitations of time and gravity I know for a fact we would all have been, even at the age of twenty something, so much more excited.

But. Alas, this is 1957 we're talking about. Surely, though, anyone capable of travelling back in time fifty or so years must have registered resentment if not total disbelief when confronted by the ease and comfort of road travel in those leisurely, rageless days. Well, to start with a driver could cross London from north to south, east to west or indeed any way he fancied totally without charge. (I know. You're already salivating, but there's more.) He could have parked for as long as he liked virtually anywhere in this parking meter-free Utopia. But of course, every silver lining has to have a cloud and in 1957 not one inch of motorway had yet been laid. Such a disappointment for all those drivers who currently hurtle blissfully trouble free around the M25 twice daily. Well, in their dreams, anyway.

Back in the austere, utilitarian days of 1957 we had to wait four years for the first James Bond film, nine years for world cup glory and no time at all before the jazz movement in Britain came exuberantly of age.

So, back in the late fifties that was what we played, New Orleans jazz, but where did we play it? The answer to that is simple, logical and obvious. At jazz clubs all over the country, which meant that life as a professional jazzer just before the revival exploded into a full blown boom was spent in almost equal parts travelling, sleeping and playing. Likewise any free time we had was spent, yes you guessed it, in jazz clubs. The club scene was buoyant and expanding at such a rate that at one time there were in excess of one hundred within what is now known as the M25 circle. But no evidence, then, that the sixties would turn out to be quite as swinging as they were. In this fairly typical 'rites of passage' time and environment we were, not unlike most young people of that time, or any other time for that matter, desperately keen not to be left out and dedicated to sampling anything that might be interesting, exciting or even simply fun. So with that in mind I introduce you the Xanadu that was the Manor Club.

I've already mentioned the clubs in which we spent a large percentage of our time at work or play but I feel it only fair to point out to any readers below the age of fifty-five years or so that these clubs bore absolutely no resemblance whatsoever to music venues as we know them today. For instance most jazz clubs were held in pubs and the licensing laws in place at that time meant that, by order of some temperance, teetotal, fire and brimstone magistrates, pubs had to close their doors at ten thirty at night with the insult to injury rider of ten o'clock on Sunday.

That said most publicans had a more relaxed attitude as to what was permitted on the premises. Along with your pint of beer you could guiltlessly light up your cigar, pipe or cigarette and puff away until the atmosphere resembled that of a herring smokehouse at which point some inconsiderate or unthinking customer would open the outside door causing an insurge of oxygen so extreme that on occasion one or more smokers would be taken with a severe attack of the bends and compelled to inhale huge lungfuls of lifesaving smoke to survive. It was also perfectly legal for yokels and urbanites alike to take part in harmless and enjoyable games of chance for cash, the most popular of these quaint, harmless pastimes being blackjack, pontoon and poker. In addition, in what was to my mind a typically unselfish gesture in the direction of dogkind, it was not only those hard of hearing or only partially sighted who were allowed to take their own version of man's best friend into a pub. In fact hardly any premises I visited displayed a list of proscribed species although it was only on very rare and special occasions that I can recall anyone trying to gain entry for say, a horse or a goat. I maybe ought to point out that, until then, I had led a fairly sheltered and non-pastoral life.

It may seem amazing in these times of gastro-almost anything that the one thing most pubs discouraged their customers from doing on the premises was eating. The only provisions made for such an emergency are almost too frightening to describe. Three or four fetid-looking sandwiches were sometimes displayed in a glass cabinet with an option of fillings ranging from cheese to cheese and tomato or cheese and pickle, huge jars of eggs preserved in something very much akin to embalming fluid and, not to forget that mystical creation of Satanism, and antidote to all ills, the arrowroot biscuit. Never having allowed myself to come so close to starvation that they were my only route to survival, I have no idea what they tasted like nor, thank heaven, what dreadful deformities may have resulted from their ingestion.

It was in the back room of just such establishments that we would offer up our brand of jazz for, what I have to say, were generally appreciative and well-behaved audiences of chain-smoking, poker-playing, 1950s youth along with their assorted pets, all of whom, judging from their relaxed expressions and nonchalant behaviour, had taken the precaution of eating heartily before leaving home. Now, unless you've just flicked this book open on the train to work in order to appear urbane, knowing and, dare I say it, cool, you may have noticed that some time back I alluded to the pleasure dome that was the Manor Club followed a little later by references to the pubs and clubs in which we played. No chance juxtapositioning this, because as the jazz club was our souk so the Manor was our caravanserai. (Look it up. It makes perfect sense to me.) As I have said the pubs in which most jazz clubs were based had by law to stop serving alcohol at a ridiculously early hour and, having restricted our intake to equate with the quality of our performance, we were often, around eleven o'clock or so, our day at the souk complete, ready for a place offering convivial company, a laugh or two and a few extra pints, even. A place such as a pleasure dome, an oasis, a caravanserai. A place such as The Manor. And so it turned out that one summer Tuesday in the late fifties Terry Lightfoot's New Orleans Jazz Band had played an earthy, roof-raising session at the weekly Jazz Club held in Union Street in Barnet and trombonist John Bennett and I felt the need of some nuggets of wisdom, some witty repartee, the latest gossip and further refreshment. To this end instead of making the journey ten minutes or so in a northerly direction to Potters Bar and home, we pointed John's lovely little MGTF convertible south and sent it as fast as its little wheels would carry it to the metropolis, and in particular a turning off the Charing Cross Road, to the street door of The Manor. Without meaning to rub it in I should just remind you that in those liberal but caring days we were allowed to park anywhere we liked in London at any time so we left the car by the kerb, crossed the pavement and looked straight through the ever-open door up the eighteen or so stone steps to a dog leg in the staircase and a small landing on which stood what looked to us like an almost life-size replica of Mount Etna. I knew just before I wrote that phrase that it was beyond the realms of even humorous exaggeration, but Gerry, the avuncular club doorman, was absolutely huge and, in his shiny bikers' leathers, his fiery, Titian red hair melting down into a full beard of equal hue, anyone would be forgiven if a first glance did, indeed, conjure up the sight of an erupting volcano albeit not on quite the scale that I first hinted. Gerry's job description would, in the unlikely event that such a thing existed, have listed as his main function to meet and greet guests on their arrival and, whenever appropriate, eject any of them who became a little too rowdy or, as we said in those days, anyone who peaked too early. I have to say though that I have never spoken to anyone who has ever seen Gerry fulfil his role as chucker-out since normally a stern look or, at worst, a growl were enough to terrify anyone but an idiot or a lion tamer into a state of quivering fear or, in the worst cases, an almost coma-like silence. I did, however, on one occasion witness this jazz-loving colossus of a man shamble to the foot of the steps to help four 'tired and emotional' young ladies from their taxi and carry them, one under each arm in two shifts, up the eighteen stone steps to the landing where he politely opened the upper door and bade them all, "Welcome, ladies, to The Manor. I hope you enjoy your evening." He then went back down the steps and paid off the impatient cabby from his own pocket. A gentleman and a gentle man. Gerry was both.

Gerry was also a vital cog in the security policy of The Manor. Now, there I go again. Once more Gerry's sheer size has compelled me to write more grotesque misinformation. I'll try again. Gerry *was* the security policy of The Manor. By this I mean that I never came across anyone who had ever seen, owned or heard of such a thing as a membership card, an annual fee or even a password. This said the club, which had seating for probably a hundred and twenty or so, was never less than half full and likewise, never overly packed. How it came to possess a late liquor license, which was not easy to come by in those days, was a total mystery. Some said it was all a mix up in the surveyor's office at the Town Hall during the rebuilding of London after the Great Fire. Whatever, so long as the club served food then the club could serve alcohol. Obviously what constituted food had not been clearly defined. This last fact would have gone some way to explaining the plate of three- or four-day-old sandwiches placed compulsorily on each table with the first round of drinks ordered and never, without the appropriate inoculations to be touched or, God forbid, eaten.

Although there was, as previously mentioned, no formal list of members we customers were required at each visit to sign a form of visitors' book used as a check on those present in case of fire. This registration gave rise, on several occasions, to great hilarity due to the fact that John and I had, over the years, got into the habit of signing hotel registers while on tour using a variety of pseudonyms for no other reason than that it tickled our still very third form, sense of humour. On the night in question we decided, being in a particularly puerile frame of mind, to take the whole thing one step further and had arranged for an obliging but it must be said, highly suspicious, stranger to call the club from the box at the corner of the street and ask to speak to us under our hotel names. So it was that, at around eleven thirty, the nice young lady who seemed to be in charge picked up the phone, looked at the visitors' book and relayed the following message to the, by now, curiously silent room:

"I have a phone call for Mister Wallcarpet or Mr Yardball. If Mister Walter Wallcarpet or Mister Billy Yardball are in the club, you have a phone call."

Most of those present looked at each other in open-mouthed annoyance at this interruption and shook their heads, others carried on drinking but with a strange look of surreal bemusement on their faces, while two or three were seen to be jiggling their fingers in their ears on the assumption they had misheard. John and I though each had a hand clamped firmly over our mouths as our bodies shimmied like *My Sister Kate* in the old jazz standard or, for those of you who've already forgotten the lyrics: 'jelly on a plate', with violent but silent laughter.

As you may have already gathered not much happened at The Manor except nattering and drinking so you may be shocked to hear this very night yet another real-worldly intrusion took place. Gerry announced, without any preamble, that we should all make our way in an orderly manner down the stairs to the pavement below. Obviously the sandwiches had, all too predictably, finally spontaneously combusted. But no, this was to be, we were told, a practice fire drill, an entirely new and quite exciting event for most of us, with the exception of Algie. Algie was the venerable former bass player with the house band at The Colony Club and insisted that he had some vague recollection of just such a drill in the closing stages of World War Two. He also insisted that George the Sixth was still our monarch and that the Duke of Edinburgh was, in fact Queen of Scotland, However, yet another stalwart member seemed to recall an evening in the late forties when the entire clientele assembled in the road outside the club with several cases of whisky for some sort of a fire drill. Alas, a perfunctory inspection of local newspaper records confirmed that on that particular day the building next door but one to The Manor was razed to the ground by what was reportedly the most devastating fire London had known since the blitz. So, possibly as a fire drill just a tad too realistic.

As we shambled down the steps toward the pavement below it seemed to be unanimously agreed that tonight's drill must be the direct result of one of two occurrences. Either the club had recently been visited by an officer representing the Health and Safety Department, highly unlikely since nobody in any position of power actually knew the place existed or, far more readily believable, Gerry had had a particularly boring week in his day job. Either way as we arrived at ground level he could be heard reading from the visitors' book.

"Well... that seems to be about it. Mr Yardball and Mr Wallcarpet are, as we know, accounted for as is Mr M Mouse, both the B Bunnys, all three M Monroes and three of the four D Ducks. We can only assume that W G Grace said his farewells earlier in the evening."

The night's excitement over (although how wrong those words would prove to be), I'll just round off the bit involving the stranger's phone call. John and I were severely berated by the majority of the customers and reminded that this was a drinking club and not, as we seemed to believe, a kindergarten and that anything that interfered with that was not, repeat not to be tolerated. So once again everyone, including ourselves, returned once more to nattering, drinking and avoiding contamination from the sandwiches, by now in the final stages of fermentation. Things perked up, however, with the arrival of one Lennie Hastings, drummer, nice man, and in his own mind, impressionist. The evening was, it cannot be denied, about to move up a notch in the field of entertainment. Lennie was an amiable, quiet spoken person. Lennie was probably the best jazz drummer around. Lennie loved a sociable drink and to make people laugh. It is a combination of these last two characteristics that I shall describe under the heading 'Lennie's Lederhosen'.

After several drinks Lennie was convinced that he was, as I say, something of a Rory Bremner and far and away his and everybody else's favourite victim was the great Austrian-born exponent of light opera and lieder, Richard Tauber. For those of you too young or too disinterested to have heard of the great man, Tauber was hugely popular as a broadcaster and recording artist of the thirties and forties who triumphed at Covent Garden in 1938 some ten years prior to his death. Lennie's tribute to Tauber involved rolling up his trousers to just below the knees (remember lederhosen) to reveal socks held up by what I think would have been called suspenders. Not quite as strange as at first it may seem, since as a drummer, it was important that his socks never became entangled with the pedals that operated the hi-hat or the bass drum and this was his own solution to the problem. Removing his jacket, squeezing an old penny coin into his right eye presumably to represent the great man's monocle and then as one final and masterly stroke of disguise, taking off his wig and replacing it sideways on to create a fringe he was, in every aspect, ready to go.

It was to be presumed that Lennie had never performed his 'remarkable likeness' in front of a mirror or he would have realised from what he saw that Richard Tauber was seriously miscast as an operatic tenor and would, without a shadow of a doubt, have enjoyed a remarkable career as a circus clown. Clearly, though, in his own mind Lennie was Richard Tauber. To complete his tableau he climbed onto one of the square, four-legged tables the better for his audience to witness the uncanny transformation that had taken place. At this point it is probably quite important to say that Lennie was a little on the squat side with a lower than average centre of gravity and the feat of climbing unaided onto a table did not come naturally to him in the best of circumstances and in the guise of his alter ego it was almost beyond him. Perhaps you may need reminding that the blood flow to his feet was severely restricted by the sock-supporting suspenders, his vision considerably less than twenty-twenty due, primarily to the fringe from his wig flapping in front of his eyes, one of which, I should remind you, was rendered one hundred percent ineffective having an old penny (three or four times larger than the coin of the same name in today's money) scrunched into the socket. Add to this the ingestion of an immeasurable quantity of scotch washed down by an incalculable number of pints of beer and you can appreciate the colossal magnitude of the challenge ahead. Remarkably, to the backing track of a chorus of oohs and aahs from the spellbound onlookers he conquered the inhospitable summit of the table, raised his arms to the heavens, made one last fine adjustment to his 'monocle' and burst, yes, burst is the word, into song. No, song is not the word. He delivered in almost faultless English, "Vee are in luf mit you, mine heart und I, vee'l be foreffer true, mine heart und I." the next couplet was almost totally drowned out by the violent and untimely sound of one of the table legs snapping under the strain as the mast of an overwhelmed galleon back in the days of... well, galleons. The tabletop slid downwards forming a surface not unlike a particularly steep ski slope down which amazed and terrified Lennie who, it has to be said, at this point displayed a considerable degree of concern on his normally cheery face, slid to the unwelcoming floor, his 'monocle' shooting off across the room like a SAM missile, his toupee parachuting gently and gossamer-like to the ground beside him.

So, not the most convincing impressionist I've seen but, as I said earlier, without doubt the best drummer it's ever been my pleasure to play alongside. We can't all be good at everything we try, can we?

There Was an Old Lady Who Swallowed A Fly

I mentioned, so far only in passing, the band led by my brother, clarinettist Terry, and during the time leading up to the sixties I spent three years as a member of his rhythm section on guitar, banjo and, briefly, double bass. The reason for my swapping from one instrument to another in this way was that the band at that time seemed to change the type of jazz it played on an almost monthly basis. This inability to settle on a style be it, New Orleans, Dixieland, mainstream or whatever was at least partly responsible for the band being always popular and well placed around the top of the Championship but never quite bridging the gap into the Premier League.

The drum stool in particular was like something from a game of musical chairs with each new incumbent being replaced more often that soccer club managers in November, but upsetting though this was musically the plus side was that it gave me the opportunity to play with some of the finest jazz drummers around at the time. Until, that is, early in 1961 when I too moved on, following the lead of childhood chum, trombonist and Mr Darcy of the jazz world, John Bennett, and became a member of Kenny Ball's Jazzmen.

This move on my part came about only after I had established a feat that must, one would think, have warranted entry in the *Guinness Book of Records* no less, in that I must be the only banjo player to have shared the stage with drumming legend, Ginger Baker. Yes, I do mean the Ginger Baker who along with Jack Bruce and Eric Clapton formed the massively successful super group, Cream, and who then stormed America with his own bands Blind Faith and, later Ginger Baker's Army. Yes, this colossus among rock drummers did indeed spend time bashing woodblock and cowbell on numbers such as *The Old Grey Mare She Ain't What She Used To Be* in the rhythm section of Terry Lightfoot's New Orleans Jazz Band. (I'm fairly sure that's what we were playing at the time, New Orleans jazz that is not *The Old Grey Mare She...* etc.) I bet that clinched his audition with Eric and Jack.

Ginger's place was taken by another fine and, in another style, equally talented drummer called Johnny Richardson. Johnny was a 'Joe Ninety' and 'Action Man' figure rolled into one and his greatest offstage pleasure seemed to be pulling the leg of members of the general public. (I've just written the phrase 'pulling the leg' without the slightest idea of what it means or how it originally came about.) Is, maybe, the leg connected in some way to an area in the brain? Does some elasticated fibre run from the big toe to the left hemisphere of the cerebral cortex so that every time someone takes hold of your leg and pulls it, a sequence of nerve impulses rushes to the frontal hypothalamus resulting in spasms of hysterical and uncontrolled laughter? The answer is no, it doesn't. I just tried it and... nothing. So I'll have to carry on as best I can only chuckling, when, or indeed, if, I think of something amusing. Anyway, whatever, pulling legs was what Johnny liked doing. For instance when asked what I'm told is the most commonly asked question by fans of drummers: "What made you take up the drums?"

Johnny would turn slowly, with a maniacal ear to ear grin and, staring straight into their eyes, reply in a fiendish Boris Karloff voice, " Well, you see, dear boy, they wouldn't get up by themselves."

Most questioners would, at this stage, usually take a small step back and say "Hoomph" or something else suggesting a degree of unease. Some would, however, on the assumption that they had misheard, persevere with, "Did you always want to be a drummer?"

"No, I wanted to play the guitar, but I never had the pluck." At this stage even the most persistent of fans would edge nervously away to try his luck elsewhere wondering, I'm sure, if he were simply being taken for a ride or whether we'd just booked Johnny out on day release from some local institution. But the occasion that stays with me more than any other is the time when, asked by a 40-something lady.

"Would you give me your autograph for my seventeen-year-old daughter?"

Johnny replied without even looking up, "I'd have to see her first but it seems a fair exchange to me."

I read recently in Humph's splendid memoir of the use of the term 'million flies' as a generic name for any transport café or, as we now say, 'greasy spoon', and I believe I may be able to accept a little vicarious glory, thanks to Johnny, and throw some more light on this fascinating subject. John was driving the bandwagon down what was then the main north-south arterial road, the A1, and slowed and pulled onto the forecourt of just such an establishment when a sleep-laden voice from the depths of the bus asked, "Is this place any good, John?"

To which he received the reply, "I should think so, all those bloody flies can't be wrong."

Over time the phrase metamorphosed with use into 'a million flies can't be wrong', and finally to 'million flies' and henceforth a breakfast stop at 'million flies' as we motored south became a widely anticipated pleasure especially for any newly co-opted member of the band. Its reputation soon spread and it wasn't long before it took top spot on the essential listings of many groups on the road regardless of their musical persuasion.

Its exotic flavours and fragrances of the everglades became understandably popular among the American musicians with whom we toured in particular the members of 'Kid' Ory's Creole Jazz Band who initially felt that 'the flies' should take pride of place alongside such utterly British institutions as the Tower of London, Flodden Field and Dick Turpin's house on some sort of Heritage List For Our American Cousins. However, clarinettist, Bob McCraken and bassist, Squire Gersh were so taken by the delights produced from within its kitchen that they insisted that the coach should leave earlier and earlier each day as our schedule took us further and further up country in order to make what were sometimes quite tortuous detours for the gastronomic alchemy that was 'million flies'.

Of course the original Mr and Mrs Flies have both passed away but I am assured the new proprietors stick firmly with the secret recipes bequeathed to them with the business and are managing to maintain a similar, unique reputation.

To this day I and the other members of the sub rosa 'flies' brotherhood have never disclosed the real name or precise whereabouts of this gourmet's Camelot except to reiterate the already common knowledge that it lies somewhere on the old A1. But this anonymity has not been easy to maintain in the face of promises of vast sums of cash or sexual flavours (maybe that should be favours but let's push the envelope a little, whatever that might mean). One ex-musician talks of having been offered 'something from Buckingham Palace' in exchange for the information. Others report instances of medically and physically inhumane treatment in an attempt to acquire the truth. Indeed, as I understand it, fingernails have been drawn, soles of feet beaten and, with total disregard for the Geneva Convention, one poor soul was even exposed to twenty-four hours of non-stop music by ABBA. What barbarism. But then how valuable the ultimate prize. It is reported that throughout this ordeal the, by now, quite aged victim would reveal only his name, rank and number. Old habits die hard. I shall, though, offer one tiny clue in this Bacchanalian labyrinth. All those years ago 'million flies' also offered overnight lodgings in two large dormitories out back and though, after several hours of non-stop driving through all kinds of conditions, we were occasionally tempted we fought that most human of yearnings for sleep and warmth on the basis that the likelihood of the rest of the insect population displaying the same admirable degree of discernment as the flies was liable to be more than a million to one.

Along with Johnny and myself the rhythm section was completed by double bass player, Vic Barton. He was a competent player in what would a little later be described as the 'trad' style, laying down a constant almost robotic beat doing a great deal of what was known as 'slapping' the bass. That is instead of simply plucking the string with fingers of the right hand he would use a pulling action rather like a bird pecking at its food generating a bass note and, simultaneously, a rhythmic click as the string hit the keyboard. This action, along with a rigid four in the bar banjo style became the hallmark of most of the bands trying to create an 'authentic' New Orleans sound.

Enough of that. Vic was a physical and hugely energetic player with an equally huge capacity for pints of draught bitter.

Now, within that short sentence is encapsulated the origin of what became known amongst the members of the band as the Ritual of the Robes.

If I'm not mistaken you have already calculated that the expenditure of a large amount of energy coupled with an ever increasing need to rehydrate the body with equally large amounts of fluid must create... perspiration. Or, as Albert might have put it... $(E+H_2O+E$ equals... Sweat$)$. So inevitably at the end of every concert Vic's stage suit would magically transmogrify from solid to liquid form and in this soggy state it would be zipped into its cover and stored in the band bus.

Now then, picture, if you can (or indeed if you even really want to), the scene in the dressing room the very next evening. Most of us are sitting around in our stage suits, sipping a pint, maybe tuning our instruments or just chatting in the knowledge that at any moment now it will begin. Yes, it's time for the Ritual of the Robes. Vic takes his suit gingerly from its cover. I must stress gingerly not in order to preserve the material but gingerly as in not wanting to gash a finger on the suit's now dangerously sharp edges. I should maybe have mentioned earlier that Vic's diet consisted of a full English breakfast, twelve pints of beer and several packets of salt and vinegar crisps daily. The result of the intake and later expulsion of vast quantities of liquid and salt had the effect of converting the suit from its most recent state to one as solid as a tabletop. The garment was removed, as I said, with great care and its two parts were held up one in each hand by another member of the band, according to an ancient arcane roster and the ritual would commence. Vic would approach each item carefully, and if the truth were known a little fearfully flourishing a bespoke, hand-tooled implement named the Robe Paddle and proceed to thrash the rigid raiment for some ten or fifteen minutes using an action not dissimilar from that employed when beating a carpet until it took on once again the reasonably malleable consistency resembling that of some sort of, let's say, 'wood-cloth', whereupon Vic would then climb or, on some occasions when we were running slightly late, be manhandled into the outfit and proceed to carry out a series of pre-ordained balletic stretches more usually associated with a row of slender, and altogether more easily bendable, girls at the bar. (I know, fresh young girls and sweaty chaps, not nice is it?) He would then head snap, crackling and popping like a whole box of Rice Krispies to the bar, and his first pint of the evening.

All, you might think, perfectly reasonable. But... ballet stretches? When was the last time you saw a double bass player executing anything even vaguely like an entrechat on stage?

The above ritual was I'm afraid a nightly one and as a consequence Vic went through more stage suits than the average musician but, ever mindful of the old wartime order to 'Waste not Want not', his outgoing suits were numbered in chalk, pinned up in a hotel bedroom and used for darts practice.

Well, that's the rhythm section accounted for and those of you who haven't been skipping too many pages should have picked up on the fact that, at that time, we used just the three-piece rhythm section without a piano. So, now that after just a few pages you've all become aficionados in various jazz styles, I shouldn't have to say that we were going through a 'back to the delta' or New Orleans phase musically.

The front line (and for anyone who's just opened the book at random I'll add that that's the group of wind instruments at the front of the band, hence, front line) in addition to Terry on clarinet was completed by Phil Rhodes on trombone via the Ceramic City Stompers from, not surprisingly, Stoke on Trent and Alan Elsdon from Highgate. Alan was a fine trumpeter in the Louis Armstrong mould and during the tour we did with the 'Kid' Ory band the equally legendary trumpeter, Henry 'Red' Allen, rated Alan among the top players around at the time. Praise indeed. I can remember Alan saying back in the 'olden days of yore' as we now call the sixties that in his opinion there was not a single jazz trumpeter in the world who had not been influenced in some way by the playing of Louis Armstrong and even today I would go even further and suggest that claim could relate in a lesser way to anyone playing any jazz instrument.

I recall Alan as a nice man with an infectious if slightly unmanly giggle poles apart from the deep throated chuckle of his idol, Satch. Somehow, and it's still a mystery to this day as to how, Allan had a more than average grasp of what is known as cockney rhyming slang and would often pepper his conversation with it in a surprising and often quite disconcerting way,

121

particularly in front of strangers whose reactions varied from an assumption that he'd just got off a plane from Eastern Europe to the more pragmatic, 'Pissed again'.

As I understand it rhyming slang was devised by London cockneys as a way of talking to each other without other people understanding and worked something like this.

In order to say the word teeth in secret a popular and wildly known phrase of two or more words was found that rhymed with the word in question, in this case teeth. A phrase that all Londoners would know would be Hampstead Heath. The rhyming word in the phrase would then be left out leaving just the word Hampstead. Ergo, instead of saying teeth the word Hampstead was used instead. Alan's conversation was strewn with such words as 'minces' equating to 'mince pies' or eyes, while 'sky' represented 'sky rocket' or pocket along the same lines 'Barnet' would mean hair as in 'Barnet Fair' (incidentally a nationally known horse fair in Victorian times). Phil told me this story no more than five minutes after it occurred. So here goes.

The band had played our first set at the 100 Club in Oxford Street (formerly the Humphrey Lyttelton Club) and, using the 'musicians only' back steps we removed ourselves to the nearby Blue Posts pub for a half hour break. Within a few minutes Alan was seen hurrying from the pub in an agitated state. Phil, who remained chatting in the club for a few minutes, then went to the gents by the back steps and came across Alan and in reply to his enquiry as to what had happened got the following hurried but matter of fact reply.

"Well, I'm up in the rubba with a nice pint of pigs when this girl orders a large gold watch, a fine and dandy and a half of laugh and titter. She then slips and pours the whole lot over my whistle. So, I went to the jam jar, got a new pair of rounders, came down the apples, cleaned my daisies and Alberts, gave my Germans and boat a quick lemon, now it's back up for a swift Vera Lynn and super. See you later."

Apparently it's quite usual to use either one word or sometimes both when talking with 'foreigners' as Alan called them. Phil is adamant that at no stage from start to finish did

Alan take a breath and when confronted Alan said that was often the case when he got flustered and he wasn't really aware of it at the time.

I presume you all managed to interpret that from my detailed instructions earlier on but for those who may have missed a word or two here's my translation.

Rubba-dub-dub	Pub (or also club)
Pigs ear	Beer
Gold watch	Scotch
Fine and dandy	Brandy
Laugh and titter	Bitter
Whistle and flute	Suit
Jam jar	Car
Round the houses	Trousers (I know, but what other word is there)
Apples and pears	Stairs
Daisy roots	Boots
Albert Docks	Socks
German band	Hands
Boat race	Face
Lemon squash	Wash
Vera Lynn	Gin
Supersonic	Tonic

If you are one of the sad few who had already correctly translated over fifty percent of these words and phrases I have just one message. Seek some sort of counselling or, at the very least, widen your circle of friends and get out more.

Those Were the Days My Friend

In 1927 a young trumpeter player scarcely as old as the century led four other talented musicians in a recording session that produced the first of a series of tracks which laid down the gold standard against which most of what we later came to know as traditional jazz was to be benchmarked. The other musicians on the first session were Edward 'Kid' Ory on trombone, clarinettist Johnny Dodds, Johnny St Cyr on banjo and the pianist, Lil Hardin later to become Mrs Armstrong. Around this time 'hot jazz', that is improvised small group jazz, was taking over the popularity previously reserved for the almost fully arranged music of the big bands and these sessions became best remembered by the name of the band involved. This band was Louis Armstrong's Hot Five and these tracks and some subsequent recordings have been known ever since at the Hot Five and Hot Seven sessions. If this seems a little overly serious on my part please bear with me as it has a considerable relevance to the denouement of this chapter. These, then, were the tracks that finally launched small band jazz into orbit not solely across America but also to Europe and beyond. But before we get too deeply into what I know to be very much an acquired musical taste I should, perhaps, draw your attention to the equally cathartic impact of two more records issued some twenty-five or so years later that stood the British music scene completely on its head. Within an eighteen month timescale a somewhat portly American singer and band leader sporting, would you believe, a kiss curl, and another US newcomer, this time with a quiff and sideburns crashed into the British musical psyche and straight into the newly established British Hit Parade. The title of the first of these tracks was *Shake, Rattle and Roll*, the second *Heartbreak Hotel*. The two singers, as if you hadn't already guessed, were, of course, Bill Haley along with his band, The Comets, and the solo sensation of the century, Elvis Presley.

So far as this country was concerned this marked the birth of Rock and Roll and whether we loved it or loathed it we all owe it a huge debt of gratitude for condemning the sort of inane popular music that had preceded it to the great sheet music shredder in the sky. If you think that's a bit unfair then muse for a while as I introduce you or, in some cases, remind you of just a fraction of those musical gems from yesteryear. Great favourites among the weak-minded of all ages were some delightfully entertaining releases by two falsetto piglets known as Pinky and Perky, not to mention their main rivals for our hearts and minds, The Chipmunks. Now is it all coming back to you? I feel I have to say that however much kudos we heap on the people who were responsible for breeding these creatures, ten times that amount must surely go the way of their patient, long-suffering and probably quite smelly vocal coach. What? You can't believe they were real animals. Oh dear. Now you've ruined the memories of all those who, as toddlers, only wanted to cuddle them. *Gilly, Gilly, Ossenfeffer Katzenellen Bogen By The Sea.* If you ever sang along to that one with Max Bygraves I firmly believe you should be roasted on a spit and served as burgers. Yet another Bygrave offering in similar vein was *Why does Everybody Call Me Big Head?* Which alluded, I think, to his role in an extremely popular BBC radio series called *Educating Archie* which stared ace ventriloquist, Peter Brough and his friend and dummy, Archie Andrews. Now then. Those of you who have been paying attention, and I can't seriously blame you if you haven't, but those who have may well have noticed the two words in the last sentence 'radio show'. Please feel free to correct me if I'm wrong. Oh, sorry, you can't, can you? But is, or is not the talent of a ventriloquist to be ascertained by just how little he moves his lips when his dummy is seen and heard to be speaking? (It's starting to look to me that there can be little to choose so far as animation goes between the man and his wooden friend.) So, what's it all about, Alife? A fully grown male adult stands in front of a microphone, one foot resting on a chair so that his 'partner' can sit at mike height on his knee, trying to prevent his listeners from seeing his lips move, particularly when the dummy is talking and even more so when the human is saying 'gread and gutter' or better still when he's drinking a 'gottle of geer'. But this is radio, for heaven's sake. Nobody is bothered whether his lips move. Nobody gives two hoots whether Archie is on his master's knee or locked away in his suitcase. This is radio. No one would have complained if he'd thrown off all his clothes and run naked round the studio. Because NO ONE COULD SEE HIM.

But, back to the music (if that's the right word) of the fifties. Let's see just how many of these you will own up to remembering: *Bibitty, Bobitty, Boo, Feet up Pat Him On the Po-Po, I'm a Lonely Little Petunia in an Onion Patch* (you would need to be almost Jurassic to recall that one), *Oh, Nicholas Don't Be So Ridiculous, Where Will the Baby's Dimple Be?* and, finally, that smash hit of 1954, *The Little Shoemaker*. In order to preserve my credibility as a serious writer, I shall resist the temptation to write 'that last tune was a load of old cobblers'. I could go on like this ad lib and almost literally ad nauseam, but in the belief that writing down your problems can help to exorcise your demons I think I'll reserve the rest for such a time as my need for therapy is even greater than today.

A couple of instrumentalists, or rather I should say instruments, from even further back that, achieved great recording success around this time were *Tubby the Tuba* (No comment) and *Sparky's Magic Piano*. I understand they eventually teamed up with *The Little Drummer Boy* to form a trio which they took on the road, but I must say I've not spoken to anyone who ever heard them in the flesh, if that's the correct term, so I can't say just how good, or otherwise, they were.

At around the same time television, too, was having a few teething problems. Top ratings usually going to variety shows such as *Café Continentale* (you can tell how continental it was from the fact that it had an 'e' on the end) and *Rooftop Rendezvous,* both of which featured leggy but thick thighed dancing girls, plate spinners, people with unnaturally bendable bodies and a nice lady who tore telephone directories in half. Children's television was even less rewarding, dominated as it was by a black and white mule who danced on the top of a piano and whispered into the ear of the lady on the stool. Yes, you have it in one, *Muffin the Mule*. At the risk of litigation I'll leave it at that.

With the general downward spiral of morals and ethics throughout the viewing public it was only a matter of time before the inevitable happened. One of the top shows on national television featured a group of virile and nubile men and women who donned pairs of white gloves and cavorted around the set clearly enjoying themselves a little too much for most viewers. But no. this was not, as you would be forgiven for thinking, an early Danish pornography channel but none other than our very own *Black and White Minstrels*. We'd stare enraptured week after week as 'Mr Interlocutor' argued with 'Tambourine Man' while the rest of the troupe performed such traditional Negro spirituals as *Oh, Dem Golden Slippers, De Camptown Races, I Used to Kiss her on the Lips But Now it's All Over* and, of course the great Paul Robeson classic, *My Girl Lives North of the Border But Last Night She Came Across*. Okay, I'll confess. Only two of dem songs were ever featured in the show and I'm sure it's obvious which dem two am.

I'm fairly convinced that in this chapter I'm starting to sound a bit of a misery when nothing could be further from the truth. It's simply that there are certain things, and I'm sure this is true for everybody, that just, how shall I put it? Get right up my nose, and not just within the music scene either. Take, for example, the complete abandonment by media folk, politicians and football managers alike of any attempt to speak the English language correctly. For example why is it assumed that the words 'phenomena' and 'criteria' can be used as either plural or singular nouns. If that's the case what precisely is the meaning of 'phenomenon' and 'criterion'? In the same vein when, exactly, was the relevant edict passed and ratified which said that the past tense of the words 'bring' and 'buy' would be henceforth mutually interchangeable. For instance, 'Only food brought in this café may be consumed on the premises'. Which means just the opposite of what was intended. Then there's the proud mother who boasts, 'I bought up all my children in London'. Did she get them as a mixed lot at Sotheby's? Or snap them up at a knockdown price in Camden Market? That sort of thing makes me sick as a parrot. Then there are the people, as I said, in the media or politics who must realise that it's a fair bet they will be obliged to use the word 'nuclear' on a fairly regular basis yet still insist on pronouncing it 'nucular'. I'm not exactly over the moon about that, either. As good as old Magnus used to say, 'I've started so I'll finish'. What about the snotty-nosed muppet who claims in that incredibly proud and superior way that he 'doesn't suffer fools gladly'. All he's saying, in reality, is that anyone who disagrees with him is a fool. But, ready for this? Here's my pet dislike with regard to our remarkable language. Who was it that decided and when that the lovely little possessive adjective 'our' must henceforth and without fail be replaced by the offensive, guttural and, frankly foreign sounding noise, 'AHR?' There is now not a single person in the media (the single of which is, of course, medium) who still recognises that the word is spelt O-U-R. Should you doubt me on this one, and I realise that you may have some justification to do just that since I may have on occasion not always been totally truthful, not to say frank, with you. But, should you not be convinced by my comments so far, listen carefully when watching TV tonight and every time you hear the word pronounced correctly as 'our' take a big swig of your Merlot. But, take my word for it you're in for a dry old night.

Of course everyone has the right to like or dislike absolutely anything they choose and I have to say that British jazz, when it finally blossomed, was not to everyone's taste. In fact some jazz purists and critics labelled it... 'a pale imitation of the original'. Of course, as I say, we all have the right to our own opinion but over the years I've met and played with several jazz originals such as trombonist, 'Kid' Ory, banjo player, Johnny St Cyr and trumpeter and jazz legend, Louis Armstrong and to a man they had only praise for the British bands around at the time.

So, run that past me again.

Some jazz critics and purists hated what we played.

Three members of Louis Armstrong's original 1927 Hot Five loved it. Yeah! That's a really tough call.

If my memory serves me correctly, I'm fairly certain that... Right. Let's hold it right there if you don't mind. I knew even as I was writing that opening line that I was making an assumption of truly gargantuan dimensions. (Even here and now today I can't remember what I had for breakfast just forty-five minutes ago.) To make such a supposition would be on a par with, let's say, assuming that Scotsmen really can play football or that Oscar Wilde was not even slightly gay. It requires the same Herculean leap of faith as the proposition that Tiny Tim was a singer or that Ringo Starr could actually play the drums. That said, I'll try the opening again.

On the assumption that my memory is as bad today as it was at the time I first began to compile this anthology of quaint Norfolk ruminations then I'm definitely not sure that, somewhere along the line I may possibly have mentioned the parlous state of the British hit parade in the nineteen fifties and early sixties. What I am, however, positively certain of is that the very first hit parade in this country, incidentally it was a Top Twelve, to be compiled from the sale of records as opposed to sheet music, was published in November 1952 and the first number one was a song called *Here in My Heart* performed by Al Martino. (I must ask you to bear with me; after all I did spend some time writing quiz books.) I know I'm dribbling on and on a bit but all I'm really trying to say is that having talked a little about some of the records of the period I'd now like to look, if I may (ahem) at the other main form of our in-house entertainment, the radio.

Among the most popular of the shows broadcast on the Light Programme (Radio 2) was the forerunner of that bane of all places of work, lifts and shopping malls... MUZAK. The programme was called *Music While You Work* and featured various bands of the day who had taken and passed their BBC audition (imagine such a thing nowadays) breezing their way through a selection of past and present pop songs to keep the good folk in the factories and on the production lines happy, loving their work and therefore earning lots of loot for their bosses. After a while, though, and in spite of its detrimental effect on profitability, the workers insisted on being paid. So started the downhill spiral in the quality of public service broadcasting. Another attempt at subduing the nation's restless workforce was an early radio version of *Britain's Got Talent* broadcast live from the canteens, chill out zones and pamper spas of businesses the length and breadth of the country and entitled, in that jolly, supercilious way so often associated with the Beeb, 'Workers' Playtime'. Along with sundry singers, ventriloquists and magicians, several of the comedians who enjoyed huge success on the Empire Theatre circuit and who would rely heavily for their humour on catch phrases would top the bill on this and other live shows. One such entertainer would, for instance, begin his act on stage or on radio with the hilarious line, 'The day war broke out my missus said to me...' and so on and so on. Another would grab the mike and yell in truly Stentorian tones, 'Can you hear me, mother?' Bernard Miles would perform his radio routine in full country yokel garb including smock, fustians and straw behind his ear and would close his act without fail with the lines, 'four seeds in a'ole, one for the rook, one for the crow, one to rot and one to grow. That's all ladies and gentlemen, goodbye'. He survived these ordeals for many years and to his eternal credit went on to found almost single-handedly the wonderful Mermaid Theatre. Other acts who would mesmerise the workers as they munched away on their Spam sandwiches were five chaps including one midget who played mouth organs called 'Morton Fraser's Harmonica Gang', a band called, 'Felix Mendelssohn's Hawaiian Serenaders' and my own particular favourite, 'Big Bill Campbell and his Rocky Mountain Rhythm'. So, as you must have already discerned for yourself, all pretty anarchic not to say subversive stuff.

As if we regular radio listeners were not spoiled enough, in 1951 along came what was to become the most listened-to comedy show of all time when a group of three writer-performers took their idea to the hallowed halls of the all-pervasive BBC. I like to think that the meeting between their representative and the BBC's commissioning editor may have gone something like this.

BBC: "Well now, what exactly happens in this, this, what is it? This go-on show?"
REP: "No, sir, it's the Goon Show."
BBC: "Yes, of course it is, goon show, go-on show all much the same, eh? So, what actually happens?"

RE: "Well, sir, the three performers are a dumpy Welshman with a maniacal laugh, a less than stable trumpeter and a comic from the Windmill Theatre."

BBC: "I say that's a nudist show, ain't it? Well dodgy start there then, my boy."

REP: "It has characters called Bluebottle, Eccles, Major Bloodnok and Grytpype-Thynne,"

BBC: "Yes, that's all very well but what goes on?"

REP: "Well, your Lordship, they all speak in silly voices and say such hilarious things as 'No more curried eggs for me' and 'I've been hitted. You rotten swine' and then there's that great line, 'He's fallen in the water'."

BBC: "Yes, yes, yes, that's all very well as I say, but what happens?"

REP: "Well, that's about it really."

BBC: "I see, well I'm going for a nice round of golf. Why don't you go away, take a little nap and see if you can come up with an idea for a comedy show for radio? Eh? What?"

The 'improved' proposal soon became, as I said, the most popular comedy show on radio and the three writers and performers (I know there were four at the outset but Michael Bentine, for reasons never disclosed at the time or since, left the show after less than two years) even bludgeoned their way up the hit parade with the unforgettable *I'm Walking Backwards For Christmas Across the Irish Sea* and, in 1956, *The Ying Tong Song*. And why not? Harry Secombe, the dumpy Welshman, later enjoyed a successful career on the West End stage in such shows at *Pickwick* and entered the top twenty in 1956 with *If I Ruled The World* from the show and, in the sixties, *This is My World*. The comic from the Windmill was, of course, Peter Sellers, whose later film successes included *Dr Strangelove*, *The Pink Panther* and *Being There,* for which he won an Oscar for his starring role. The less than stable trumpeter could never be anyone other than the wonderful Spike Milligan. Spike had several unpredictable TV series and a successful career as a writer, his best remembered work being his autobiography entitled *Hitler, My Part in His Downfall*. His final and most typical piece of creative writing, however, appears on his headstone. His epitaph reads quite simply, 'I told them I was ill'.

I believe we should remind ourselves that broadcasting in the early fifties was still very much live and therefore open to all number of hitches, glitches and gremlins as well as risk taking or even abuse by those wielding the omnipotent mike. A serious offender in this respect was I'm told one Max Miller otherwise known as 'The Cheeky Chappie'. Cheeky being, in this case, hugely euphemistic, risqué or outright blue being best descriptive of some of his gags.

Max, along with one or two others at the time, seemed to find the power that goes with an open microphone irresistible and would often overstep the mark to some extent, but on one occasion he totally obliterated the mark with one mammoth rush of adrenalin (or could that be alcohol?) to the brain. His radio career was forced into a lengthy sabbatical when on one broadcast he closed his act with the following rhyme, 'When roses are red they're ready for plucking, when girls are sixteen they're ready ... Cheerio, ladies and gents, cheerio'. Needless to say he received a severe dressing down, a BBC ban and almost certainly some years on the naughty stair.

Now then, if through a deficit of either years or, more worryingly, fully active memory cells, this brief recap of fifties and sixties radio humour means less than nothing to you then I have to say you have my deepest sympathy not to say sincerest condolences, particularly if your earliest recollection of childhood humour originates from television. There can, in my humble opinion, be little or no comparison between the two media in the realms of original comedy. How, I ask you, can a programme about a family of subterranean, litter collecting creatures, and I use the word in its most offensive meaning, with names like Orinoco and Uncle Bulgaria, live in the same universe as Bluebottle and Eccles? How on earth can Dougal, Zebedee and Florence, not to mention a snail called Brian mutter things like 'Time for bed' and expect to raise a titter from anyone who recalls Major Bloodnok's urgent, heartfelt outburst, 'Quick nurse, the screen?' Where, I ask you, is the humour to be gained from two flower pots and a weed, a postman and his cat, an engine called Thomas or a construction worker known imaginatively as Bob? The answer is that those lucky souls who can recollect Eccles in search of the Chinaman, Ar Pong, knocking on a door and asking, as it is opened, 'Are you Ar Pong?' only to get the answer, 'Yes, we are Ar Pong to five o'crock everly day'. Those privileged people fortunate enough to have inhabited this sub-world of fifties radio broadcasting are blessed indeed, and will forever be rounded, grounded never astounded folk with the exception, that is, of those 'too happy few' constrained under the Mental Health Act.

Sadly you would need to be sixty plus to have remembered the Goons' first time around and several attempts have been made to imitate or replicate the show but all have turned out to be only slightly better than bog standard. (A masterly segue indeed from comics to bog standard. Unbroken, logical and seamless, totally the reverse of the rest of these ruminations).

However, I need to ask you, at this stage, to think very seriously as to the genesis, the where and the how of the phrase 'bog standard'. Was it, you may think, something to do with the magical, the mysterious, the overpoweringly smelly peat bogs of the Emerald Isle? Does it owe its origins to the crude, coarse-sounding reference, in some places, to the toilet as the bog?

Let me put your mind at rest. Its creation lies in neither of these interesting but simplistic suggestions. So, settle back, turn up the hearing aid and I shall reveal all.

Right at the top of every boy's wish list in the fifties, apart from five minutes of wild sweaty sex with Marilyn Monroe, was the Hornby electric train set. (Personally, even at the age of fourteen I would willingly, even eagerly, have abandoned the train set in exchange for a whole ten minutes of Marilyn's time, but then I never was much of a one for trains.) It just so happens that the very same Mr Hornby of the eponymous train was also the producer of third choice after M M and the said choo-choo, and that was an evil, dark, satanic piece of apparatus called the Meccano building set. This was a nerdish, mummy's boy sort of toy consisting of lengths of green metal perforated end to end with tiny nut and bolt holes about a quarter of an inch apart from which the dedicated students of engineering, who didn't for whatever unnatural leanings fancy Marilyn, could happily build cars, trains and other exciting things. This spoilsport of a hobby soon became as popular among pre-teen boys as 'Men Only' and 'Tit Bits' and soon top-up kits could be purchased to expand the creativity of those sexually repressed anoraks who, for whatever strange reason, just couldn't get enough of the thing. These add on kits were supplied wrapped in thick, shiny paper for the first few years but eventually along with almost everything else, with the possible exception of Irish haute cuisine, they surrendered to progress and introduced the two kits in boxes. (So, do I have to tell you anymore? Have you had a really rough day at the office? Is your wife's affair still playing on your mind? Are you still hitting that smelly, dark, unctuous Australian merlot? In that case I'll give your brain a rest and fill you in.)

Now the eager not to say desperate Meccano builders were offered there extra parts as, 'boxed standard' or 'boxed deluxe'. So 'boxed standard' or bog standard as it soon became was second rate. But I can hear you thumping the book on your knee and shouting 'What about 'boxed deluxe'. Well, as a result of the humour and ingenuity of the British joking classes, never ones to miss an opportunity of slipping yet another smutty phrase into our noble, nay stately language, the words underwent a devious not to say convoluted transposition and became, the opposite of 'bog standard' and therefore the acme of excellence, the pinnacle of perfection, the very height of heavenliness. I do believe you have it, yes… 'the dog's bollocks'.

I'm sorry for the Anglo Saxon word at the end there but to be honest I don't much care for the word 'canine' and 'cur' seems somewhat affected so 'dog's' it has to be. Now then, earlier in this rumination I remember speaking however briefly about some of the comedians and humorists from our not too distant past and I must say that while researching the subject, (yes, I know it may not seem like it, but I have tried) it struck me that the impression most commonly held of the people who made us laugh on stage or radio is that of a clique of mean, morose and often quite intolerant members. I must say, though, that my own opinion is that anyone who can stand alone in the spotlight and try, sometimes against some pretty stiff opposition, to make us laugh night after night, deserves to be allowed to behave just exactly as they please in their private lives. That said, throughout the fifties and sixties our band worked with a gaggle of the country's finest comedians including the likes of Tommy Cooper, Frankie Howard, Jimmy Tarbuck and, of course, Morecambe and Wise and I'd simply like to put on record that whatever they got up to at home they all struck me as being normal, grounded professional entertainers.

Over the years I've gradually come to realise that a lot of the things that made me smile, odd phrases, anecdotes, jokes, that sort of thing have been part of conversations that I have, how shall I put it, overheard? That is to say I was there among, or on the periphery of, the main group not exactly taking part in the chat when I just happened to overhear a word or two that led me to believe I was about to hear something of interest to my slightly unusual sense of humour. One such conversation took place at the circus ring of all humanity, a jazz all-nighter. I was with the Cy Laurie band so it has to have been 1953 one Friday night at Cy's own club in Windmill Street in London's West End. We played our last set and I was listening to a new semi-pro band trying, maybe a little bit too hard, in the soul-destroying 4am slot. The fact that it was a semi-pro band is just about all I can recall and that only comes to my mind because I can picture them and how smart they looked having come to the club in their day job clothes whereas we full time jazzers (I was still at school) had all day to scour our wardrobes for the loosest, thinnest, grubbiest and coolest layer of clothing we could find. If you've ever been to an all night jazz session you'll have a good idea what I'm talking about if you haven't let's just say it could be a bit on the steamy side.

Anyway, I sense that I am rambling a bit so I'll get on. I was stood behind an old sofa, beer in hand listening to the band when I started to catch snatches of conversation between the two female occupants of the couch. One was a bit, well how should I put it? ...Tarty. Indecently short skirt, T-shirt, no bra, purple nails and hair to match. She turned towards her neighbour who was, it seemed, a total stranger, in well cut trousers, elegant white blouse and expensive-looking hair and said:

'Bloody good this lot, ain't they?'
'Bloody good is exactly what I'd have said.'
'I've seen them a few times.'

'So have I.'

'I fancy the clarinet player, he's dishy ain't 'e?'

'I certainly couldn't disagree.'

At this point the purple-haired girl took a large swig from a coca cola bottle wrapped in brown paper, the club not being licensed for alcohol and pressed on.

'I could give him one, no trouble.'

'I'm sure you could.'

'He's a horny looking beast, ain't 'e?'

'Horny's the very word I'd have used.'

'I'd like to shag him 'till his eyes popped out, wouldn't you?'

'Precisely what I was thinking.'

'He's smart too, always dresses so nicely.'

'Yes he does, and so quickly too.'

Purple hair's brain was fighting hard to interpret the last reply. The inner struggle took on almost gargantuan dimensions causing her face to contort between bafflement and surprise. Suddenly the bulb clicked on and, thought lines still etched deep into her face, she replied.

'What. That means you've already shag...

'Yes indeed, many times. That dishy, popped-eyed, horny-looking beast of a clarinet player happens to be my husband.'

On another occasion I was once again at the edge of a chatty group this time at a party given bi-annually, or should that be bi-ennially? I'm the same with plants I'm never quite sure which is which. But in this case what I can say with absolute certainty is that this was a twice yearly gathering. To refer to it as a party though it is a bit like saying the Chelsea Flower Show has a few nice plants, or that Gainsborough wasn't bad at portraits or even that Puccini didn't have a bad ear for a tune. It's really not a good enough word. However on this particular day the food, the wine and the company were all of the usual high quality and everyone was perfectly relaxed. I was, as I said, on the fringe of a group of four or five friends and acquaintances and the topic of conversation was dogs and dog breeding.

Now then, I should perhaps point out at this point that my mind has a habit of suggesting something amusing whenever I hear what sounds like an unusual but perfectly correct phrase and mostly I just smile inwardly to myself, but on the odd occasion the impulse to speak my thoughts aloud gets the better of me. I began picking up the conversation at a point where one of the group was talking about the possibility of reintroducing a bloodline in animals after a break of several years. It was suggested that sperm from a good dog could be stored for a number of years and that when required the semen could then be used to impregnate a suitable bitch and bingo. Away you go. One of the group confirmed this saying:

'Yes, I know someone who re-launched his line using some twenty year old semen.'

The temptation was far too great to quash so I chipped in.

'They'd be Petty Officers, probably.'

Nothing. Just silence, several blank faces all turned in my direction as at some mystifying and totally unfathomable piece of modern art.

Unable to stop myself I then exacerbated the crime by adding.

'I mean the twenty year old seamen would have more than likely been Petty Officers.'

Still in absolute silence their faces now showing a cross between bemusement and sympathy the group moved as one person to re-form the circle and the chat continued.

'Well, yes as I was saying, this friend of mine...'

It seemed a good time to smile and help myself to another plate of tiramisu with a little piece of Pavlova and maybe, just maybe a tiny sliver of trifle on the side. Mind you, knowing our hostess that would have meant one and a half units of alcohol to tick off against my daily allowance so maybe not. Then again there's always the other approach that says, sod it, why not, you're only young once.

My next tale was also overheard but I'm unable to say who by because I can't for the life of me tell you who related it to me or even, in all honesty, when. So, let's pitch it somewhere around the middle of the sixties at the entrance to one of the hundreds of jazz clubs that had sprung up cloned, seemingly, each one from the other right across the country. On the whole these venues were run in a strictly business-like way with just a little bit of leeway thrown in. This last phrase meant that most promoters, providing that they were already filled to bursting, would allow the odd friend of the band in for nothing. Gratis. On the house. So this is what I was told even though I cannot attribute it to anyone in particular.

Just after the interval a Scandinavian student with only a tenuous grasp of the English language addressed the club promoter thus.

'Good day, sir, I have been told to tell you that I am a friend of Zartrun Bonpley and that I do not have a need to pay.'

'I'm sorry mate, I've never 'eard of 'im.'

'But you must know him, he said I was to tell you I am a friend of his and you would be pleased to invite me in.'

'Like I say, I'm sorry mate, but Mr Bonpley don't play in this band, this band's all English with English names.'

'But he called me last night and said to me to say I am with Zartrun Bonpley, I do not understand.'

'I don't know how many times I need to say this but there's no Zartrun Bonpley in this band. Anyway what's 'e look like.'

'He is very high and thin and he has, how you say, a beard like a big bush.'

'Well, I dunno, I suppose that could be Al Baker, he plays trombone.'

'Ah. Yes now you have it what I am saying to you, I am with zer trombone player.'

Whether the promoter let him in or smacked him round the ear I've no idea. I leave it up to you to choose.

I'm not too sure how long ago an event has to have taken place to qualify as a reminiscence but I'm pretty sure it's ok to relate a misunderstanding, the outcome of which, when I told it to my wife, made us both laugh animatedly enough to cause people to start to stare. We were sat on the patio of the café area of a large and busy garden centre, where only minutes earlier I was involved in this conversation. We'd decided on a couple of baguettes for our lunch in the café of what was, as I've said, a bustling and fairly noisy garden centre. My wife was investigating the pros and cons of sitting in or out on the sun-drenched patio area and I was at the till about to pay. The nice lady at the till said, 'Nine pounds eighty, please.' And I in turn handed her a ten pound note at which point she asked, 'Are you sitting in?' I replied in all honesty. 'I'm sorry but just at the moment I haven't got a clue. Does it matter?'

'There's a ten percent discount if you are.'

I turned this piece of new information over for a while wondering, as I did so, why you would be charged less for sitting in the already overcrowded café as opposed to the almost empty and temptingly quiet patio area. Still puzzled I enquired. 'Sorry, what was it you asked again?', to which she replied, a noticeable hint of tetchiness creeping in, 'I said, are you a senior citizen?' Suddenly the whole of the previously quiet surreal exchange slotted perfectly into place. The lady smiled sympathetically saying, 'Your change, sir.'

Smiling though she was I could read the words clearly etched behind her eyes that said:

'Poor old sod can't even remember how old he is.'

Well, I did say at the start that it was a noisy place and it's an easy mistake to make.

I'm stretching the postcard a bit with this final example of humour overheard as opposed to simply heard although in this case I'm certain that's exactly what was supposed to happen.

In between the final rehearsal and the recording of one of just dozens of Morecambe and Wise shows on which the band appeared on something of a resident basis Eric was standing at the bar with a small group of friends including the show's writers, Sid and Dick, and was trying to gauge their responses to a few gags that he would use later to relax the studio audience just before the show started. One or two of Ken's band including myself were stood just along from the group and it was impossible not to hear what was going on and as I said that was, in truth probably the point. Now then, whether there was more of this first gag I can't say but I don't think it matters too much. This is where we came in and I feel obliged to say, as they do on TV 'The following contains strong language and scenes of a sexual nature from the start'.

Sid said, 'Well, if you're supposed to be a pirate captain where's your buccaneers?'

To which Eric replied in that high-pitched, strangulated voice he used. 'One on either side of me buckin' head'.

On the assumption that some of the less sensitive among you are still with me, I'll continue.

Eric. 'Tell me Doctor, I'm ninety-two and I've married a young girl of nineteen. Is it okay for us to have sex?'

Doctor Dick. 'Of course. But you must be careful. With the age difference sex could prove fatal.'

Eric, after some consideration. 'That's too bad. But if she dies, she dies.'

Eric, to everyone in general in his best female voice. 'Dear Aunt Sally, I can't stop my husband having sex with me. He grabs me in the kitchen when I'm washing up. In the lounge when I'm dusting. Even in the garden when I'm weeding. No matter what I do I just can't stop him. What do you advise?'

Ps. I'm sorry, but there's nothing I can do about the wobbly writing just at the moment.'

I can well remember how we and just about everyone else in the bar fell about laughing and to me it illustrates just how humour has changed in, what I've just realised, is almost half a century. Although, I have to say I've tears of laughter in my eyes right now so maybe it doesn't.

She Wears Red Feathers

In the mid sixties the Kenny Ball Band's third or fourth trip to America was for five jazz club dates before flying on to New Zealand for a twenty-nine day concert tour. Jazz clubs in the United States were very different to those we'd been used to playing in the UK in that they were primarily subscription affairs whose members tended to be mainly professional people older than the fans back home. After the final American date which was at the Fire House Club in San Francisco, where incidentally the only means of entry to the stage from the dressing room above was down a fireman's pole, we flew to the town of Suva in what was then the British Crown Colony of Fiji and an evening playing for the Ambassador and his guests. As if such a gig were not in itself exotic enough we flew from there straight to Honolulu in Hawaii for three days rest and recuperation at the remarkably luxurious Waikiki Beach Hotel, not something, I'm at pains to point out, that we did on a fairly routine basis. I'll not upset you too much just in case you're reading this during yet another grey, wet, windy and cold English summer but the whole island was exactly as it was in *Hawaii Five-O* ('Book him, Danno', what a great series that was.) only warmer. On our first evening, rested, relaxed and pink of flesh four of us met in the hotel bar for a few beers and a natter. Since this is America we're talking about it wasn't long before we were joined by a charming, amusing and garrulous GI called Luke or to give him his proper title, Sergeant Luke of the US Military.

Approaching midnight we'd all phoned our wives, enjoyed the day and had a pleasant evening's chat and were probably feeling at one with the world when Luke offered the following anecdote. Take heed before you start though as I shall ask two questions after the finish.

Luke had a cousin called Chuck (what else?) who like our new friend was also from Texas and also like Luke lived in the

141

state capital, Dallas, and it has to be said Luke's accent was hugely reminiscent of that of one J R Ewing whose shooting on screen is probably as well remembered as the death, in the same city, of John Fitzgerald Kennedy. Chuck had qualified as a veterinary surgeon and worked at a small animal practice in Dallas with, as you can imagine, mainly pampered pets with equally pampered owners. It appears that a couple of years previously he and his family, dissatisfied and uncomfortable with city life, had agreed to uproot everyone and everything so that Chuck could follow his dream and accept an offer of a post with a small town practice in the foothills of the Catskill Mountains in New York State. Here his patients would be more varied and decidedly larger than those in a city like Dallas.

Chuck and his family absolutely loved it. Clean air, mountain breezes and friendly and accommodating townsfolk. After maybe a year or so Chuck was approached by a posse of town dignitaries including the senior partner in the practice and asked if he'd like to take part in a bit of fun and undergo some sort of initiation ceremony in order to acquire a certificate and recognition within the town that he was now an honorary 'mountain man'. Having discussed it with his family they agreed and a few days later he was collected outside his house by a half dozen 'good ol' boys' from the committee and driven, amid assurances that it would be a great laugh, a little higher into mountain country. As they drove one of the group, the leader of the contingent outlined for the first time what it was that Chuck would have to conquer in order to be accepted as an honorary 'mountain man'.

"Now then, Chuck," he said, "what we'll find when we reach our destination will be a clearing in the woods, at one end of which you'll see a vast, dark cave and at the other a simple shack. Now then, in the cave lives a nine foot tall grizzly or as we say around here an 'ornery big ol' bar'. In the shack there's a wizened old hag of more than a hundred years old. To prove you could survive as a mountain man you need to strangle that 'ornery ol' bar' with your bare hands (bare this time rather strangely pronounced, bare) then you gotta have full sex with that ugly old hag. That clear?"

Just as Chuck nodded reluctant agreement they pulled into the clearing. Sure enough as they disembarked a deep, thunderous growl came from the cave. Chuck pulled back a little, one half of his mind telling him he couldn't turn back now for the sake of his future and that of his wife and children. The other half telling him it was all some terrible dream and he'd soon be laughing his head off. Either way he regretted bitterly not asking for details of the challenge before agreeing in what was, he now conceded, an ill-considered and bravura way. He'd told his wife and children he'd do it and they'd told the other school moms and kids. So, only one way to go. Thoughts of his family imbued him with a new feeling of resolve and determination and he leapt from the car and strode off toward the cave of the 'ornery big ol bar' intent on not falling at the first hurdle. Soon he disappeared into the stygian darkness of the cave and almost at once the whole clearing was filled with the most dreadful, the most unnatural shouts and bellowing as man met bear. Some minutes later the terrifying furore came to an abrupt end and Chuck, clothes and body caked in blood, dirt and gore re-entered the daylight. He strode confidently to the assembled group, some still covering their ears against the earth-shattering onslaught.

His only words were, "Well, that's that. Now, where's this old witch you want me to throttle?"

I said at the beginning there were two questions to follow. Firstly Dallas is not the state capital of Texas. What is? And secondly when, precisely, did you realise Luke's story, rather than being an anecdote was, of course, a joke? Bearing in mind that we were all somewhat 'relaxed' at the time, by the time I fell in Chuck's physical health and, in particular, his future sex life were in very grave danger. Nevertheless, I can remember quite vividly almost choking to death as I took a large swig of Southern Comfort just before his final question. I realise that the whole episode in the bar at the Waikiki Beach (I just had to say it again) took place over forty-five years ago now (did it really, surely not, where did all that time go?) and that the joke has probably circled the world several hundred times since, but way back then it was all still new to us and as a man we literally fell about at the end. I also beg no forgiveness for including what is

143

simply a straightforward joke on the grounds that it is one of my three favourites of all-time. As I'm certain you have realised there's only one left to go.

The state capital of Texas is, as I'm sure you knew to a man (and I know that's sexist but you understand perfectly well what I mean) Austin.

I was making my way to the bar in search of one for the frog (remember the good old rhyming slang? Frog and toad... road) when Luke announced to any or all of us: "Listen here, guys, I've had a terrific time tonight. How about I return the compliment and entertain you all where I work. Maybe tomorrow. What do you say?"

We'd all had nights on military bases before and to be honest the thought of hundreds of lads drinking till they either fell over or brought it all back up had, strangely, long since lost its appeal.

Ron was first to reply, "Sounds like fun to me, Luke, but I really must write a letter home, sorry."

Luke persevered, "What about you, John?"

"I really should get some trombone practice in, it's a nice offer, but thanks, anyway."

Luke began to grin at this stage and turned to Dave questioningly.

"I hate to spoil the fun but I really must get a bath and cut my toenails, you know how it is."

By now Luke could scarcely contain his amusement. "Say now, Paddy, I suppose you'll be tuning your banjo, getting your hair cut or something. Come on, guys, give me some credit. I'm not asking you to the base for the evening. Guys just get drunk and whistle and holler there. I want you to come where I work weekends, that's just about the best striptease bar on this island. There the guys get drunk and whistle and holler too, but at least you get to look as some female flesh, what do you say?"

As it turned out, Ron had written home just that day, John could soon fit in a bit of practice some other time and Dave decided his toenails weren't really that long anyway. So we all agreed to meet there in the bar tomorrow evening, went through some strange ritual where you try and smack each others' hands in mid-air and crept towards bed.

The following evening we all five (I've remembered now the ritual the previous night also involved asking people to 'give me five'. Sorry to interrupt but it just came to me.) met up in the bar at the 'smartest hotel in Honolulu', fell in behind Luke and walked the four hundred or so yards to the strip bar where he was employed at weekends to work the door and generally make sure the evening never got out of hand. I think we'd call him a bouncer. He said we could take our pick between Chief of Security or, as he preferred, Controller.

The club was oval in shape with a bar across the length of one end and a stage across the other. In between were around fifty or so round tables all groaning under the weight of bottles, jugs and cans of some stuff called 'Schlitz' or 'Budweiser' which Luke advised us was the best American beer you could buy. (It's happened again, the good old oxymoron has raised its head. 'Best American beer' simply does not work. It's like saying the 'finest Icelandic haggis' or the 'best Brazilian Morris Dancer' or even 'gourmet German cuisine'. It just does not exist.) Around each of the tables were four or five GIs having a great time, but taking absolutely no notice at all of the entertainment taking place on stage. The production line of strippers was made up of a mixture of girls of all ages from all countries and of all sizes. Generally speaking, though, they could all be described by the selection of adjectives in *vogue* at the time, including buxom, curvaceous, cuddly and Rubenesque. Nowadays they'd be classified uncompromisingly as... fat. They were accompanied, if that's the word, by a gentleman of around eighty years on the drums and what looked to the practised eye to be his father playing some sort of keyboard which sounded at times remarkably like a good old banjo (any remarks suggesting yet more oxymoronism will be severely frowned upon and totally ignored). In order to take into account their venerable age and the accompanying frequent lapses of memory or concentration they had clearly unilaterally decided that the choreography of each consecutive 'exotic dancer' was perfectly suited to the music of *Hey, Big Spender,* which they played throughout the entire evening starting back at the beginning with the arrival on stage of each new performer. New perhaps not being the most appropriate word.

So we settled down in a booth to one side of the room to take in the show joined by Luke who, in his own words, 'only stepped in if things got out of hand' and so far they seemed to be going quite smoothly. Smoothly, that is, until the arrival on stage to the strains of *Hey, Big Spender* taken from the top of course, of Jane. Jane, I have to say was not fat but was most definitely overweight. If that sounds odd it's because Jane's arms, legs, torso and head were pleasantly slim. Her chest, however, most decidedly, was not. Those before her had displayed bosoms ranging from voluptuous down to, well, almost nothing, in fact one poor girl was so lacking in the bust department as to prompt Dave to comment that she looked as though she had two backs. In Jane's case nothing could be further from the truth. The technically precise size of her chest was certainly not for me, or indeed any of us, to speculate on but her initial appearance on stage prompted an excited cry from the crowd to the effect that, 'If those are forty-six I'll eat 'em'.

Whether Jane was happy, or even prepared for her bosom to be chewed on will never be known. Not so the fact that she was new to the striptease scene. That was obvious from her response to the whoops and whistles that accompanied the speculation as to her exact measurements. Clad in nothing but a G-string she displayed all the inexperience, learned quite quickly by other girls of, shall we say, larger than average bustlines, in acknowledging her reception by taking a bow. Now then, let's just recap on precisely what we have here. A girl with a heavier than average top half has lent forward and in her excitement at the applause has totally forgotten everything she learned at school about, yes you've got it... gravity. The poor girl plunged forward ending up flat on her face on the stage. For some reason this prompted dislike verging on hatred and loathing for the clown who, in the eyes of everybody else, had caused this catastrophe by remarking loudly on the possible size of her bust. There's no polite way of putting it. All hell broke loose. Punches, cans, bottles and chairs. All were thrown wildly and, it must be said, aimlessly as every one of the members of the audience seemed to be fighting everyone else. No sides were formed, no enemy identified, no rules of engagement established. Bedlam, chaos, pandemonium, mayhem. Take your pick. On stage the band, both of them, were crouched behind the keyboard instrument until a rocket-propelled table smashed it to firewood provoking that sad, deflating sound so beloved of film-makers. Fearing for their lives they dashed. No, that's not the word. They sped. Wrong again. They shuffled, yes, that's the word, they shuffled for sanctuary in the dressing room. Meanwhile, Jane had, with one superhuman heave, managed to get to all fours, but the effort and emotion required proved just too much and the poor girl slumped forward to her original prone position. On the floor of the club two or three hundred GIs were battering the living daylights out of one another, bottles and cans were crashing into the side of our cubicle. Luke put his head round the end of the booth and snapped it back just in time to avoid being decapitated by a slightly subsonic table. All the time he was laughing fit to bust prompting Ron to ask whether maybe he should try to intervene. Luke shook his head and chuckled. Eventually two MPs, attracted by the furore fought their way into the club and managed to get Jane into a sufficiently upright position before easing her gently off stage. Luke, still laughing out loud, persuaded us that we'd probably be safer outside and in answer to John's question of just who paid for the enormous amount of damage not least to the club's furniture and décor replied, "That's easy, every week the owner sends an inflated bill for the cost of replacement, sets about sticking the chairs and tables together and pockets whatever's left. So, the club owner and the CO of the base are both happy. The proprietor for the little extra income, and the CO for having it all take place somewhere other than on his camp."

We all nodded and grunted agreement and Dave, surprise, surprise, had to have one last taunt. In as close to an American accent as he could get he called out as we left the premises, "They're sure as hell forty-six. I ate 'em last night."

A spontaneous broadside of cans, bottles, chairs and even a sadly battered snare drum crashed into the door as it closed behind us.

Outside on the pavement, we all shook hands with Luke and thanked him for the entertainment. John suggesting that he might now need to get back inside and start doing a bit of 'controlling' in line with his job description.

"Hell, no. I only step in when it gets out of hand. Tonight's only Friday. It don't get out of hand till Saturday."

Dance of the Hours

I'm absolutely convinced that ahead of our first trip to America in 1963, I had, like most people I suppose, already formed my own idea of what the average, run of the mill, man in the street ordinary US Joe was liable to be like. I'd seen enough TV and films to know that, for instance, the politicians were all aggressive, blustering, filibustering, self-centred opportunists and that the stars of Hollywood male and female alike had all undergone frontal lobotomies and had, each of them, a buzzer labelled 'Tears' stitched into their undergarments especially for award ceremonies or in response to any questions regarding dogs or their co-stars. (I'm sure this is superfluous but I feel I should point out that I mean to suggest co-stars of the Hollywood actors not the co-stars of the dogs, but you do have to be so careful in these litigious times.) What I was not totally prepared for though was my initial confrontation with the cult of the smile. Americans seem to have this innate conviction that nobody can possibly dislike you if you simply present them with the perfect smile and, by and large, I saw absolutely no reason at all to doubt this presumption. In fact so important is it considered that you are preceded through life by this all-embracing smile that a surgical procedure has been developed whereby a set of braces can be attached to a baby's teeth while it is still in the mother's womb. I should say that in general the new mother's pride and joy at the birth of her beautifully braced bundle of happiness, in most cases, was hugely outweighed by the pain and suffering involved in breastfeeding.

To us Brits this non-stop, coast to coast smiling fest may seem just a tiny bit well camp if not insincere, but to Americans it seems rather a demonstration of instant recognition and affection not unlike when a poodle humps your leg or a baboon bares its backside. What is says is, 'Hey there, buddy, I come in peace, I like you and maybe we could get to know each other even better'.

But, what the hell? I liked the Americans that I met and found that they normally meant what they said and that a smile and a handshake could make you a friend for life. I even managed to get used to being told by the waitress in the diner to 'Have a nice day, now' when just ten minutes earlier we'd been total strangers. One problem I did have trouble with though even in this atmosphere of openness and truth was just what was expected in reply. Sure, if you were on your way to a nice day's shopping or sightseeing or you were meeting your mistress in a motel in ten minutes you could truthfully and comfortably say something like 'Why, thank you, I'll sure try'. On the other hand, if you were meeting your tax inspector after lunch or, worse still, you'd made up your mind to end it all at two o'clock by jumping from the fortieth floor window, 'Gee, thanks and you too,' wouldn't feel absolutely comfortable to me. What do you think?

No, I find no problem whatsoever with being told to have a nice day after all isn't that just what we'd all like? But the next giant leap for mankind from here is just more than I can swallow. Who on earth thought that 'Missing you already' would sit comfortably even with those gushingly sentimental Yanks? Surely it's taking things just a little too far, do you agree? Good. So, now back to the diner. Picking up my tab (that's American for paying my bill, I've talked like that ever since my first visit) she gives me my change and before I can even turn towards the door says, 'Missing you already'. What's that all about, Alfie? We haven't just made passionate love. I've not just told her she is my world but that I am catching a flight out in an hour never to return. I've said good morning and drunk a cup of coffee, for heaven's sake.

It was this particular year or it may well have been the one after that we flew on from the USA to Australia for a short concert tour of around ten days or so and in the arrival lounge at Sydney airport we were each interviewed for local radio and in response to questions about music and hobbies and that sort of thing we all gave predictably diverse answers, but when our tastes in humour were mentioned both John and I expressed a keen liking for the latest LP by the American comedian, Bob

149

Newhart along with others such as Allan Sherman, then thought no more of it. Bob Newhart was best known in the UK for his recent albums of one-sided conversations, that is to say he would talk to someone who wasn't present and we the listener had to assume the response. Now I'm not too good at this sort of thing and to be frank it's so long ago my memory's not all that clear but it is essential that I give you the gist of at least a couple of tracks. One, for instance, involves a driving instructor (Newhart) and his passenger (let's say Mrs Cook) on her very first lesson. A typical Newhart line might be, 'Yes, you're right, Mrs Cook, now that we've actually stopped on the traffic island, it would be a good time to learn reverse gear'.

On another track a submarine has resurfaced just off Hawaii following several weeks of manoeuvres in the Pacific and the line is, from the Captain, 'Aah. Come on now, men, don't be like that. Let's hear it for the cooks'. Likewise, Sir Walter Raleigh has just returned from the New World bringing with him tobacco. The disbelieving interviewer says, 'Give me that again. Walt. You roll it up in paper, you put it in your mouth and then you do what to it?'

For you to commit the gist of these lines to memory would be a great help later on but that's just the beginning. Another of our particularly favourite humorists was a man called Allan Sherman who besides selling lots of LPs also made the UK charts with a single called *Hello Muddah, Hello Faddah,* the title of which is the first line of a letter from a young, inept and fairly precious Jewish lad on his first day at summer camp to his parents. Here's the difficult bit. I can tell you that the tune to the song is that of *The Dance of the Hours* by the Italian composer Ponchielli. And am almost certain that all of you (that's maybe just a tiny bit optimistic), I'm fairly sure there are one or two among you who will know the tune but can't connect it with the title. So, no help there, then. To make it fair for everyone what I shall endeavour to do is to convey to as many people as possible just how the melody of the first couple of lines goes.

So then, those of you who have in the house a guitar or piano (that's the big cabinet in the front room with a bowl of fruit on top, or if you're posh enough to own a grand piano then it's the small shed around which the front room was built) please

150

locate and identify them, now. Thank you. Some of you may possess alternatives such as a ukulele, mandolin or, if yours is a truly discriminating household, a banjo. Dig them out, this is where you finally learn to play a tune. In your search you may come across assorted keyboard instruments. If these are reasonably in tune, fine. Do not, however, under any circumstances consider resuscitating something called a Stylophone. You'll know it as it will have a picture of Rolf Harris on its top. Reason enough on its own to discard it. This contraption had in its day less of a claim to be a musical instrument than the bagpipes or tambourine so should you unearth one during your search give it to the young lad with instructions to chuck it in the first skip he comes to on his way to school. Failing that, on the assumption that you were sufficiently feeble-minded to have bought one some forty or so years ago I can only assume that you are, by now, absolutely gaga, in which case give it to the nice man in the white coat when he comes round to see you after lunch. He'll know just what to do with it.

So, now we've dug out all our old banjoleles, lutes, mandolins and guitars. In fact any fretted instrument (that's anything with a long neck divided into sections with lengths of metal and, before you ask, no, that doesn't include a Masai tribeswoman) in almost any state of repair just so long as it still has at least one string and a bridge. Starting at the top of the arm and that's the end nearest the pegs, number each of the sections marked off on the keyboard from one through to, let's say, fourteen. This last number being sited very close to the body of the instrument. This is best achieved using either chalk or numbered sticky labels but if, for whatever reason, neither of these is available you might like to chisel out the numbers using let's say… a chisel. Stage two. By pressing a finger of your left hand onto the string at any space and plucking the said string with a finger of your right hand, produce a note. (Should you be one of those spooky, annoying people who insist on being left-handed simply read left for right and vice versa.) It really is simple from now on. In your own time and at your own tempo (pace or speed) move the relevant finger of your left hand up or down the fingerboard (fig 2) in the order the numbers are shown on the plan and continue plucking. In order to simplify the whole exercise I have intentionally ignored such things as a clef, a time signature, a key signature, rests of differing values to the notes, so just give each of the notes the same length and, as long as you follow the numbers correctly from beginning to end, you will in no time recognise the tune and be dancing round the room singing, "*Hello Fadduh, Here I am in Camp Granada.*"

By the way should this first lesson prove so irresistibly inspirational that a few of you follow your dream and become great classical guitarists or, indeed, concert pianists, I feel that it would be in no way inappropriate to offer thanks and public recognition to your very own Svengali. To square your conscience you may well wish to divert the odd recording royalty this way too.

That's the stringed instrument dealt with. The procedure is even simpler for those of you with a piano or other keyboard instrument such as the harpsichord or spinet. (Before you start getting above yourself and protesting that the piano also has strings and should, therefore, be included with the others let me stop you there and point out that a piano also has hammers and on that basis is most usually classed as a percussion instrument. So just hold your horses for a while.) If any of you should, by some stroke of luck, uncover a spinet, even a harpsichord gathering dust in the attic or garage you might consider getting in touch since I have a nephew in antiques and I'm sure he would be prepared to take these old, outdated items off your hands for ten or even fifteen pounds each. But I digress. Number your white keys as for the guitar from the paradigm below starting on a key directly to the left of a pair (not a trio) of black notes and follow the order of the numbers given. You will, in a matter of minutes, recognise the melody and may like to adjust the value of the notes to better suit the tune. So, there. You are now all sufficiently musically accomplished to join in the singing when we finally get to the end of this tale (fig 1).

Play: 3 - 5 - 5 - 6 ----- 6 - 8 - 8 - 7 ----- 5 - 6 - 6 - 7 ----- 5 - 11 - 11 - 10

Fig 1

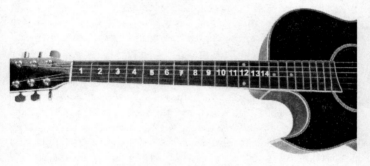

Play: 1 - 4 - 4 - 6 ----- 6 - 9 - 9 - 8 ----- 4 - 6 - 6 - 8 ----- 4- 14 - 14 - 13

Fig 2

I should I feel, at this point, say that in the unlikely event
that a few of you may not be able to find a suitable instrument of
any sort or, indeed, having followed the instructions to the tee
still have no cognizance of the tune in question then you'd better
ask Grandma to run over it a few times for you on her trombone.
Drastic, I know but I see no other suitable solution. Okay. So
back to the saga. Oh, by the way just one more word of advice
before we do actually proceed further. Under no circumstances

should you try reading and practising your instrument at one and the same time in that headlong rush so typical of today's impatient and dilettante approach, since it is altogether too much for a person in your delicate and, frankly, worrying condition and will all too quickly cause your feet to swell and your brain to hurt, at which stage you must stop at once and take around a half hour nap followed by a steaming cup of beef tea and fifty or sixty press ups before eventually continuing with this account.

Well now, let's see. Oh. Yes, John and I had discussed on air our particular fondness for the humour of Bob Newhart and Allan Sherman and, as mentioned earlier, thought no more of it. That evening we played a concert in Sydney and after several encores (No, that's not just swagger and conceit, it happened and I intend wherever possible to record the truth and that's all there is to it.), we were gathered in the dressing room which was fortunately larger than usual for there seemed to be half the audience there too. We signed photos, chatted and answered questions as best we could and as the crowd began to thin and the room cleared a voice was heard above the general hubbub saying in the appropriate American accent, "Give me that again, Walt. You roll it up in paper, you put it in your mouth and then you do what to it?" It was quite chilling. It was as though the man himself were there so uncannily accurate was the voice and intonation. "Come on now, men, don't be like that." This as a solo and then three voices in unison, "Let's hear it for the cooks." It turned out that this lad, a bit younger than us, was an ex-pat Brit working for a big Aussie company. So taken was he by the Newhart style of humour that he had committed to memory several complete albums track by track. As we stowed away our instruments and suits he rattled off line after line in a remarkable replication of the original, ending each amid gales of laughter from John and me. So entertained were we and taken with his youthful enthusiasm that we invited Nick to travel with us in our coach back to our hotel where, having washed and having had a few beers, we all planned to visit the local jazz club where one of our favourite Australian bands was playing till two o'clock next morning. Back at the bar we were once more entertained by Nick's incredible impersonations and memory. But, after a while this incessant droning, as it was now beginning to sound, seemed to pall a little but, despite one or two discreet hints, the outflow continued unabated. Now some of our favourite comic's work was beginning to be annoying, not only for us but for the other lads too. We had, at this stage, long since ceased to join in the punchlines but his persistence was as unflagging as his skin must have been thick. About this time our roadie, Bill, came round and suggested we should move towards the coach as time was passing and we had pledged to show up and hear our mates play. Right about now Nick decided he needed the loo and headed off to the gents. In one fell swoop we were all on the coach and away. Harsh? Yes. Uncaring? Probably. But we had another couple of hours of meeting people ahead of us and Nick was now monopolising the centre of attention. We talked on the bus and at the club bar and John and I decided we'd done the right thing however callous it may have been for, to be honest, he'd just become a bit of a nuisance. John and a few of the lads had a sit in with the locals and soon a great atmosphere developed in the club which was heaving with people. I ordered a couple more beers, left them on the bar and made my way to the 'dunnie'. (I make that four languages so far, but who's counting?) As I was washing my hands John walked in and did the same in the neighbouring sink and the conversation went like this. (Well, not quite yet because first I'll give you a little challenge. With the evidence you've had so far how do you see this tale concluding?)

Okay. That's long enough, now on with the conversation.

John:	"You'll never guess what."
Paddy:	"No, I'm sure I won't."
John:	"I've just been talking to Nick."
Paddy:	"How on earth did he get here?"
John:	"He reckons he ran it. Gotta be two miles or more. Told the guy on the door he was in the band and just breezed in. He said he was sorry he'd missed the signal at the hotel and so he made his own way."
Paddy:	"Missed the signal? Blimey that was the whole point. He's just become a burden. Although he is good."
John:	"He certainly is and, come on, he's just a lad enjoying his fifteen minutes of fame."

155

At that point the door creaked open and "Ah. So, this is where you are?"

We looked at each other, shrugged our shoulders and grinned, bracing ourselves.

"*Hello Muddah, Hello Fadduh.*" Just one voice.

"*Here I am in Camp Granada.*" A veritable choir and, if you all joined in too that means that just about everybody had a good feeling. Everybody, that is, except Signor Ponchielli who was positively whizzing round in his grave.

A Foggy Day in London Town

For me 1957 was a year of anticipation and expectation. I'd completed my National Service, celebrated my twentieth birthday and achieved my ambition of joining a professional jazz band. Not much, then, to upset the apple cart or darken the horizon you might think. That's what I thought too but I hadn't reckoned with something that had become the bane of the lives of anyone whose work, or indeed pleasure, involved driving in or around London particularly at night and even more particularly in winter. This something was called SMOG.

Smog was a combination in both name and reality of smoke and fog and on many occasions it brought the capital and probably most other major cities to an almost total standstill. It has to be remembered that clean air was not something seen as being in any way important or even desirable and factories were allowed to belch out their smoke by the ton; smokeless fuel was not something many city dwellers aspired to or even thought about, in fact I'm not even certain that it had been invented, and almost all forms of road transport spewed their exhaust fumes willy-nilly into the atmosphere. I said almost all road transport because there were a few exceptions. For instance the bicycle was a great example of non-polluting transport but these were about as common on the streets of the metropolis as were for instance 'coloured' policemen or bendy buses, not to mention aerially propelled families of hogs, sows and piglets. So, not many of them, then. There was, however, another form of what might be called inoffensive transport and this may come as some surprise to the toddlers and memory-challenged older folk among you, and that was the good old reliable, always on time, non-fuel consuming (except for the occasional bag of oats) ...horse. Yes, man's second best friend was still to be seen pulling the brewery dray, the rag and bone man's cart and the milk float around the streets dispensing as they went not one

157

milligram of toxic waste into our environment. (The London to Brighton stagecoach, too, having only finally ceased its healthy forays in the years directly following the Second World War.) I realise that some among you may have been a little sceptical about one or two instances that I have claimed as factual and may wish to ask your parents or, indeed, grandparents to fill in one or two of the slightly grey areas in your knowledge while those still in full-time education should, perhaps, get your Modern History teacher or PE instructor, as I believe they are now known, to give a talk or put on some sort of light show or whatever to add to the realism of what I realise must be a tricky, even pointless subject to absorb for anyone not actually there at the time.

A line or two at this point about the loveable, biddable horses who served these honest artisans so well and so unquestioningly. (Having just written it I have second thoughts about the adverb 'unquestioningly'. I can't be sure that the concept of questioning is right up there at the peak of the equine psyche. 'So, you'd like me to pull your cart around London all day? Well, there's one or two issues we need to get straight first. For instance, recompense. Apart from this bag of stuff normally only eaten by men in beards and ladies' skirts, what's my rake-off? And time off. When do I get to visit my family and my friends at Ascot? Then there's the question of retirement. I'm not going to put up with any old field; I'll need a nice shelter and regular visits from a bit of female talent. I'm sure we don't need to spend too much time in smoke-filled rooms to reach some sort of agreement here'.)

All things being equal and an agreement reached, it should be pointed out that these sweet and amenable creatures were responsible, in a way, for their own particular form of pollution.

Several times a day but particularly just after a bag of Celtic breakfast they would, only naturally, need a toilet break, although not to put too fine a point on it they would simply do their business in the road and quite often at the trot, if you'll pardon the expression. Not something likely to cause too much of a stir you might think but those old wartime invocations still rang loud and clear in the minds of your average townie in those happy but frugal days. Who can forget the poetic resonance of

'Coughs and Sneezes Spread Diseases' or the intellectual conciseness of 'Waste Not, Want No?' but the message that seized the nation's imagination was that most agrarian of instructions, 'Dig for victory'. And dig for victory they did. Not just through the straitened years of the war but onward into the following decade of celebration and renewal. And so it was that the bucolic citizens of our capital city became hooked on horse manure. Not in those days the multi-use composts, the Blood Sweat and Bone or the wonder chemicals Sulphate of Ammonia and Nitrous Oxide. The latter not noticeably increasing the vigour of plants but at least giving them a good laugh. No, the only fertiliser with an unblemished success rate, the droppings that had defeated the Luftwaffe, the poo that had terrified the Third Reich, the dung that had seen us through the Blitz had been supplied for nothing, free of charge by the patriotic, the unselfish, the conveniently xenophobic good old English carthorse.

It seems almost unbelievable now, here in this most technological of times, that men would place such a value on something so simple and basic as horse manure. But take my word for it grown men would follow these proud beasts around their suburban roads armed with shovel and bucket all the quicker to get the steaming package back home and on to the tomato patch or the rose beds. Several times though this otherwise harmless pastoral pursuit would explode into violence as two or more growers would face each other over a disputed pile and a modern form of jousting would take place, each knight armed only with a shovel and protected only by a bucket. Though usually resolved without too much blood and gore, so highly prized was the grail that one or two of the not-so knightly gardeners would resort to underhand tactics which included the purchase of double sized buckets and the mixing of some form of purgative in the noble creature's nosebag in order to produce a heavier or more regular motion. A ruse left over from the darker days of the previous decade.

There. You see? I've done it again. My intention was that these few pages would be about our experiences of 'the Great Smog of 57' and here I am rambling on about horse manure. I think someone's been messing with my medication again.

So here we go again. At its worst the London smog, or for that matter the smog in any other major town or city, was not only unhealthy to those forced to inhale it such as pedestrians or cyclists but it could be literally fatal for car users left sightless by its density. So dense and impenetrable could it be that vehicles' lights, in our case the bandwagon, were totally ineffective being simply reflected back by the sheer blackness rather than piercing it. On these occasions our only response and, as I was to soon find out, that of many other road users, was for someone to walk in front of the vehicle and, with the help of a torch, to signal if it was going up the kerb or just as likely into the back of another car or, worse still, lorry of bus.

On the night in question we were trying to get from the Hampton court Jazz Club to Potters Bar, marked on the map in those times with the legend 'Here Be Dragons' and where uniquely five of the six members of the band (TL's N.O.J.B. at that time) resided within a few hundred yards of each other. As I remember John Bennett, the band's trombonist, was at the wheel and it was my turn to take on the almost suicidal role of vanguard. Experience had taught us that it was advisable, even essential, in view of the dreadful Stygian blackness of it all, for the man at the spearhead to wave a torch from side to side behind his back in an attempt to guide the driver while at the same time showing some kind of light to oncoming vehicles, equally likely to pop up on either side of the carriageway or, indeed, the pavement. So disorientating was the utter blindness of that awful night that I had displayed a bicycle lamp clipped to the front of my duffle coat. (A description of this wonderful but strange piece of clothing can be found in the Glossary of Terms.) You will, by now, have worked it out, being an erudite, perceptive, not to say cutting edge sort of person, that speed was a rare commodity on these occasions, rather progress of any kind was almost non-existent, our rate being something around two miles an hour on a straight road. However, with visibility around five feet (which, incidentally was the distance between me and the band wagon) it was impossible to tell whether we were on a straight road or travelling the wrong way up a pedestrian shopping precinct. So it was that the initial few minutes of my watch were anything but auspicious since after only a couple of paces I collided head on with a bright red pillar box and only narrowly avoided being crushed from the rear by the very vehicle I was meant to be leading. I ran around the wagon to make sure all was clear (quite a joke really since visibility was by this time no more than three feet and the pain from my bruised ribs diverted my attention from the task at hand). After some discussion we were soon underway once more albeit slowly and briefly. Approaching what I saw as a junction I semaphored to the band bus to halt while I investigated further. (I can't be absolutely certain but I do seem to remember the words 'I'm going outside. I may be some time' passing summarily through my smog fuddled mind.) Suddenly as if by some evil feat of magic it was before me. A cross between the Blackpool Illuminations and 'The Crucifixion of Christ'. As the hideous apparition inched slowly toward me it's true, horrifying substance became clear. It was a young person serving exactly the same purpose for a busload of school children as I was for the bandwagon. We came to a halt no more than nine inches apart, me with my torch and bicycle lamp her, for that's in reality what the beast was, a halogen lamp in each hand, a belly bike lamp and, gaffer taped to her forehead, another light resembling some sort of miner's 'Davey Lamp'. It wouldn't, however, have taken a dead canary to demonstrate to her that the air she was inhaling was, at best noxious, at worst... fatal.

After a few seconds' confrontation she signalled to the minibus driver that she was about to reverse, took two steps back, signalled right and, passing behind me, was on her way followed closely by the bus she was so conscientiously escorting which stripped a length of paint from our bumper and threatened to fracture the only good leg I had left after my earlier confrontation with the post-box. Her strange but perfectly executed manoeuvre complete, I caught a fleeting glimpse of her rear just long enough to notice another lamp at her waist and yet another fixed using the aforementioned gaffer tape to the back of her head. The whole professional exercise was carried out with military precision and, I had to admit, put my relatively laid back and frankly pretty feeble attempt to safeguard the lives of my friends and colleagues to shame. Egged on and, I have to say more than a little annoyed by the whole operation and the whole affront stinging even more by having been outclassed, yes outclassed is the word, by a woman, no by a girl, I signalled my own charges to turn left and pull up while I investigated each corner in search of a street name to try and ascertain if we were still in London or had taken a wrong turn earlier placing us a little west of Margate. After a long and detailed consultation with the AA book the road signs did seem to suggest that we were still in London, but alas, not as we'd hoped in Finchley but still somewhere south of the Thames. A further piece of information surfaced during my examination of the road names and it was not something that I felt obliged to share just at that moment. It would seem we had met the illuminated girl bang in the centre of a set of crossroads controlled, or in this particular instance, not, by traffic signals. I say not controlled with total confidence since the mechanism seemed to have jammed with the lights showing green in all four directions. Now, along with other survivors, I've not often had anything positive to say about the Great Smog of 57 but on this particular night had the smog been just a little less impenetrable (I'm fairly certain deep down that that's wrong. Smog is either impenetrable or it isn't, I imagine there are no degrees of impenetrability but, to be frank, who really cares? Under the circumstances not me.) and visibility just a little better all sorts of traffic would have been crossing, or trying to cross from all sorts of directions and that nice young female 'Son et Lumiere' show and I would have been squashed as flat as a pancake. Or, to be more precise, two pancakes. The one giving off a gentle flickering glow, the other blazing garishly radiant like some thermo nuclear, radioactive isotope or something similar. I'll not easily forget that night nor the initial sight of the apparition still filed away in my memory bank under the suitable and unforgettable panjandrum 'The Trafficator Queen'.

What? No, please. Stop all that shaking of the head and sucking in of air showing doubt or non-acceptance. The word 'panjandrum' finds its way into my conversation on an almost daily basis. Well… monthly then. Okay. But I know for a fact I've used it at least once before so just swallow your pride and accept it and turn the page.

Up a Lazy River

On our second trip to the States, or maybe it was the third, no matter, we did a nice comfortable tour taking in some of the uniquely-run private jazz clubs that I'm sure I mentioned earlier. Around the middle of the trip it was nice to find that we had a little spare time in the cradle of jazz, New Orleans. I took the opportunity to stroll around the picturesque and atmospheric French Quarter and, with it's neon signs proclaiming 'Storeyville' this and 'Crescent City' that it was easy to make the half century leap backwards to those golden, creative but turbulent days of the melting pot that was the very birthplace of jazz. No effort at all was needed to recall the names that had been so crucial to my early development as the like of 'Dan Dare' or Arthur Ransom had been to many of my contemporaries. Names with the tinge of mystery and intrigue so redolent of the clubs, bordellos and 'cat houses' of New Orleans in the early years of the twentieth century. Names that created and fed my musical cravings some ten years earlier back home in suburban England. 'King' Oliver, Louis Armstrong, 'Kid' Ory, Johnny St Cyr, and the elegantly but suggestively nicknamed 'Jelly Roll' Morton. The list is truthfully endless and later, as I strolled past the legendary Preservation Hall, 'Bunk' Johnson, George Lewis and 'Buddy' Bolden and the years seemed to fall neatly into place. For me it was, and I have to say fairly unexpectedly, an awesome completion of some, bumpy and uncertain rites of passage. (I can tell that those of you who now feel you know me fairly well are maybe justifiably expecting bracketfuls of lampoon and sarcasm, but be patient and wait just a little longer. This after all was where it started.)

Later that same day I came upon something that set my mind racing along slightly different lines. The catalyst for these new imaginings was a wonderful totally and lovingly restored Mississippi riverboat moored by the jetty glistening gaudily and evocatively and boasting to anyone who bothered to look of that half-refined savage time that was America's Deep South at the turn of the century.

I can't really remember just what the boat was called but it certainly should have been something like *Mississippi Belle* or *Queen of the River* and equally there should have been a Negro jazz band playing below in the salon. Elegant, statuesque ladies in silk and diamonds and their suave but powerful gentlemen with their gold watch chains and brocade waistcoats all jostling for a place at the gaming tables or just mixing, drinking or listening to the music and thanking God they were alive. How, at that moment, I envied them.

Sad to say the only boat that we as a band got to play on, with the exception of a cruise around the Med, was a very different kettle of fish, indeed.

Each year a Riverboat Shuffle was organised aboard two sister ships called the *Royal Sovereign* and the *Royal Daffodil* from Tower Pier to Margate and, fortunately, back again. But the *Mississippi Belle* they most certainly were not. No silk or diamonds or brocade here just around two hundred or so jazz fans along with four or five bands on each vessel. The two pleasure boats left the pier about fifteen minutes apart and featured non-stop music and a non-stop bar all the way to Margate where, after a couple of hours break, the bands would transfer from one boat to another for the homeward leg so the fans got to hear every group on board. Whatever the weather the bands played up on deck and I have to say that we were usually pretty lucky in that way, while down in the bar area a selection of blues and boogie pianists worked their way through a rotating roster. On one occasion I was particularly keen to hear *Legendary Boogie Virtuoso, Speckled Red*, and was hugely disappointed to find that this was in fact yet another American pianist and not, as I had hoped, a fully trained piano playing chicken. My curiosity had been to see whether or not his legs were long enough for his feet to reach the pedals. While I'm in a very rare complaining mood, I was equally disappointed to find when ordering my first beer that it was all bottled with no draught of any sort available and even worse it was served in a dreadful plastic container (common sense must dictate that you

164

can't call them glasses for obvious reasons). Apparently, according to the bar manager to whom I complained vigorously, it was all a matter of Health and Safety. It seems that in case of trouble among the drinkers the plastic thing would not be broken and used as a weapon. As he said this, the barman pushed my half-filled glass substitute towards me along with what remained in the half-filled bottle. I don't know, is it me, or what? It would appear that while every effort is made to ensure that you are not stabbed to death with a piece of broken glass, it would be fine for you to have your skull cracked open by a blow from an empty beer bottle.

So it is that I am glad to say that over all my time afloat I never saw the slightest sign of bother. That is, not among the fans. However on one occasion some members of the crew took part in what can only be described as a mutiny and were promptly, if a little harshly, cast away on an uninhabited tropical island just off the coast at Herne Bay.

Although these trips were on the whole very well organised I spotted what, to my mind, had the potential to throw up the odd anomaly. While both vessels were alongside at Margate the musicians were allowed to transfer their gear unsupervised from one to the other in readiness for the return session. A decision to my mind reckless in the extreme and even, not to put too fine a point on it, totally irresponsible. Not the most reliable or self reliant members of the human race at the best of times, giving musicians two or three unsupervised hours to chat and drink with mates that in some cases they may not have seen in several weeks was, as I have said, to my mind one of those 'not properly thought through' concessions. A ruling similar in action to giving control of a jumbo jet to a gibbon with learning difficulties and no previous flying experience and then showing surprise and disappointment when it crashes.

Surprisingly this transfer of instruments and assorted clobber from *Sovereign* to *Daffodil* and vice versa seemed at first to be going, a little worryingly, too smoothly. You know? That smoothness and efficiency that tells you a good thing cannot possibly last. And sure enough after a couple of years the odd musician (I mean odd as in a random few not odd as in idiotic, or then again…) who should have been on the first boat to leave would arrive at the quay just in time to see his transport and, incidentally, the rest of his band, chugging off towards the Tower. At first efforts were made to address this minor hitch but, alas, all in vain. For a couple of years several attempts were made to transfer these late arrivals from one boat to the other by throwing a series of ropes between them and effecting some form of breeches buoy but far too many aspiring but unfulfilled young jazz players were lost to a watery grave before achieving their potential. So, with something like a dismissive shrug of the shoulders this practice was abandoned. I'm sure, though, that we've all heard the rumour that on Walpurgis Night as the eerie winter's mist hangs menacingly over the estuary the trained ear can pick up the strains of *Tiger Rag* wafting through the heavy, all-consuming blackness. But that's getting into the realms of fantasy. (I feel obliged to point out for those caring, innocent souls among you who, even now, are fighting back the tears over the callous loss of young life, that nobody really perished. Or even got wet. I made that bit up as a bit of a joke.) Although now I come to think of it there was the time… No, that was in a film with Kate Winslet, and, if I'm not mistaken, an altogether bigger boat. With the easy attitude of both musicians and sailors these instances of tardiness were soon assimilated into the system with just the smallest amount of reshuffling and understanding. Those who should have been on the first boat but had, for whatever reason, failed to make the departure in time would have been invited to 'sit in' with a band on the second one. Likewise those who were due to sail on the second boat but, and here's the worrying part, had actually sailed earlier than planned would follow a similar protocol. So all in all every musician got to play with someone or other and the fans got good value for their money. (If that makes complete sense to you I suggest you make an appointment to see your GP. ASAP. If it doesn't don't worry. It just means you're as simple as the rest of us.)

Laissez-faire lay back, laconic and louche. No, not you, sir. All traits that jazz musicians might be perfectly content to accept as being part of their makeup. But don't be fooled. Quite a few of them are also perceptive, paradoxical, pragmatic and, well… Peruvian. (Not the word I wanted but P is a difficult letter.) On top of all these characteristics add one more. Opportunistic.

Maybe it's something to do with standing on stage in close proximity to someone beating the living daylights out of a ruddy great drum kit for a couple of hours a night. Maybe not, but something causes a part of the frontal lobe of their brain to home in on chances more quickly than normal people. (I must say that's not an explanation I could easily accept simply because the 'brain' bit requires far too great a 'suspension of disbelief'.) Anyway, opportunists many of them are.

So once they'd all worked out the implications and potential benefits of the 'sitting in' answer to the problem of late comers they quickly began to adapt it to suit their own interests. That is to say 'side men', that's the musicians other than the bandleader, of one of the bands outside the top division would purposely fail to make it at the appropriate pier at the appropriate time and as a result probably get invited to sit in with a more prestigious group on the other boat. Not much harm done really providing you had a good enough reason to tell your own bandleader for going AWOL. On at least one occasion we were involved in just such a plot. Having played the outward leg on the *Royal Daffodil* we obediently switched our gear to the *Royal Sovereign* for the return trip. A relatively new band, let's call them Mike Davis' Stompers since I'm fairly sure there never was a band of that name, was at the centre of this affair.

Trumpeter Mike, as sometimes happens in the early, spiky, walking-on-eggs days of a new band, was having trouble developing a rapport with his pianist and clarinettist and the feelings were, or so we'd heard, mutual. It didn't help the situation any that Mr Davis turned out to be somewhat less accomplished a musician than had first been assumed. Their early weeks then had been, shall we say, less than a barrel of laughs for the aforementioned pianist and clarinet player who decided to jump ship at Margate and return not on the *Daffodil* as scheduled with their teammates but on the *Sovereign* as stowaways. We met up with them in the bar on board and soon struck up an acquaintance so that after a few numbers of our first set our leader, Ken, made the following announcement.

"Ladies and gents, round about now we're going to have some younger players sit in with us."

167

The very proud and eager young men stood in anticipation at the side of the stage.

"We're going to give our own Ron and Dave time for a quick one or two in the bar, and we have coming on now the pianist and clarinettist from the newly-formed Mike Davis' band."

The two players' pride and eagerness were not in any way misplaced. They were about to relax and enjoy about a half hour or so with the best band of its kind in the UK with the two most respected brass players around at the time. The young pianist cracked his fingers; the clarinet player adjusted his reed.

"That's not all, folks. I'm going to get a chance for a little break too because completing the line-up we have the leader of the band himself, on trumpet, let's have a big hand for Mike Davis."

Not quite the way it was all meant to turn out but, as someone once said, 'the best laid schemes of mice, men and musicians gang aft aglay'. (I'm not absolutely certain but I'd say those last three words count as language number five.)

Another bizarre episode is presently seeping into my consciousness while the riverboat trips are still fresh in my memory and it concerns someone who, rather like the legendary I P Stanley had no use for forenames. He lived in a grand house just out of Margate with views over pleasant fields and soft, rolling hills and he was known to us all as D S. The reason for this odd, almost cloak and dagger behaviour was his desire not only to maintain a state of complete anonymity but also to ensure that his association, not to say friendship, with members of that half light, half understood, half satanic world that was the British jazz scene of the nineteen sixties, should never under any circumstances become known to his family or, more especially, the board members of his company. God forbid it should actually make it into the public domain. It seems that he was a highly respected member of an even more highly respected family in the world of… no, not espionage, not finance, not gun running. His family had for many years produced brandy, which is why D S was determined to function in his own Jekyll and Hyde world not just without a Christian name, but even without a surname. Mind you once you had discounted Mr Three Barrels and Mr Napoleon it didn't take an enigma code breaker to work out that he was, in truth, D S Martell. Whoops. That's done it, Cover's well and truly blown now. We were perfectly happy to play along and were equally content to refer to him only as D S.

D S was a nice man but, of course, he was. He was a jazz fan. Older by possibly twenty years than most of us he had all the assurance and self-confidence of understated wealth and for reasons known to himself he was, not only, a jazz fan but he enjoyed a vicarious pleasure from mixing with members of that musical genre. So, it came about that, having docked at Margate one year he invited us all, including our wives, to a buffet lunch and drinks at his palatial, but tasteful mansion of a house. It was just a shortish walk from the quay and on arrival we were made extremely welcome and it was abundantly clear that he and his wife had gone to a lot of trouble to cater for D S' maverick, bohemian friends. It is not difficult, I think, to imagine that under such sybaritic circumstances both the food and the drinks were dispensed with unaffected largesse. The conversation turned from music to golf, a game at which D S was, he claimed, a keen but only competent player who practised his tee shots from his patio driving the length of his garden and into the fields beyond.

The rest of us became aware that he, Ken and our road manager, Bill, were rapt in golf talk and it wasn't long before he wheeled out his splendid set of clubs onto the terrace. Ken was soon seen pulling each wood and iron from the bag and hefting each with unconcealed delight. For nearly five minutes or more the rest of us were deeply involved in our own separate conversation and had ceased to be aware of the three golf buffs. Suddenly one of the ladies put her hand to her mouth and gasped and when we followed her eye line we too became aware of just why. I mentioned somewhere else in this book the sort of thing that can happen when those two predatory, desensitizing agents, booze and bravado, work in tandem and this was clearly one of those instances. Roadie Bill was lying in his back on the patio. Between his teeth he clasped a short white golfing tee. As we watched in what must have been the most pregnant silence imaginable, Ken placed a ball on the tee, stepped back and, without so much as a practice swing or any further ado, drove the ball with a large headed wood out over the garden and into the field beyond.

D S stood in dumbfounded silence. Bill gave a short laugh more in relief than amusement and Ken placed the club back in the bag.

D S found his voice and said, "That was pretty impressive Kenny. Do you play a lot of golf?"

Ken's reply was calm and matter of fact. "Two or three times."

D S said, "I'm surprised you can find time to play two or three times a week in your line of work."

Ken said, "No, not two or three times a week. Two or three times. I've played golf two or three times in total."

D S turned alabaster white. Bill put his hand to his face as if to feel the hole where his nose had been.

Ken finished his brandy, sat on a sofa and fell silently asleep.

If I Had a Talking Picture of You

In the year 1963 the Kenny Ball band, of which I'd been a member for around three years, entered the UK charts with an instrumental version of a haunting, Japanese song retitled with some concession to the West's limited knowledge of things oriental, *Sukiyaki*. Later that year, the single having done well in Japan itself, the band was booked for a concert tour of the 'Land of the Rising Sun', not to be confused with *The House of the Rising Sun*, which was a brothel in the Animals' hit of the same name several years later. As a precursor to the tour we went into the recording studio with our producer, Alan Freeman, and a shedload of sheet music and managed to put together an album of Japanese songs that none of us had ever heard of until that day. The LP (remember them? Big round flat things in cardboard covers) was entitled *Holiday in Japan* but was not available in this country until, and maybe one could ask the question, why, some forty-five years later.

The trip was to take in venues with, it must be said, suitably oriental sounding names such as Kyoto, Yokohama, Osaka, Hiroshima and Nagasaki, and we were all curious and excited at the chance to experience another way of life, another landscape and another philosophy; and in order to acquire a lasting record of the trip I purchased a cine camera. Before I go any further I'd just like to say that my own impression of the Japanese people that we came into contact with was of a proud, disciplined and generous people with an aura of inner self-contentment, with the exception of those we met in those last two war-torn and devastated cities where, in addition to the aforementioned characteristics, I sensed an almost overpowering sadness. Not for themselves. Not self pity. But, a sadness for us and others from the West. It must be remembered that this trip was less than twenty years after the Hiroshima bombing and its citizens had a

171

stark, poignant and everlasting reminder in the preserved ruins and the museum alongside.

So, back to the cine camera. Not to be confused with the tiny hand-held video camera so prevalent in today's world, my purchase had far more in common with, let's say, a howitzer or Gatling gun and if the truth were known probably weighed about as much as both of them put together, just a little vexing since the contraption was, as we all know, intended to be portable. But that problem paled into significance compared to the other gigantic, even insurmountable hurdle. That is, in a nutshell, I hadn't got a clue what to do with it. I'd watched those busy little Japanese people in Trafalgar Square and Soho and they made it look like child's play. (I can't imagine what they could find of interest in Soho. Coffee bars? Street musicians? Gaming arcades? Prostitutes? Oh, well, maybe we'll gloss over that bit.) I had, however, not a single doubt in my excited little mind that I would soon qualify for the 'Ars Gratia Artis' award for 1963. Why? What would give me such confidence? What would cause me to brag in this obviously uncharacteristic way? The answer was John Bennett. He was the band's trombonist and founder member as well as being a highly respected member and doyen of the circle of Potters Bar cinematographers and he had agreed to pass on his years of acquired wisdom on the flight over to the East. I cannot speak too highly of his mentoring, tuition and enthusiasm in what was, let's be fair, an undertaking that would try the piety and compassion of someone with even more patience than Job. He gave me tips that had taken him half a lifetime to absorb and hone. Things that just give you an edge in the cutthroat world of photo journalism. For instance, how many months or years would be wasted before you could learn to ensure that the lens cap must always be removed before filming? See what I mean? Invaluable. He knew it all. Always be certain that the camera's pointing in the direction of the object or person you intend to film. Again, priceless. At this rate I'd be light years ahead of all the little chaps by the time we got there.

When the day of departure finally arrived I was just about Pathé News standard and champing at the bit (I clearly don't mean that in the dictionary interpretation as 'to munch noisily' but I'm sure you get the message). However, if it's alright with you I'll just meander a little about now. (Why, I ask myself, do people say 'if it's alright with you' or 'if I may' when they're going to whether they may or not? It's the same as 'with your permission' or 'if it's not too much trouble' then they plough ahead before the subject has a chance to open his or her mouth. In my book it's insensitive verging on insulting and should be avoided. So, if you're happy with that I'll get back to the text.) Meander I said and meander is what I'll do. In fact I'd like, if that's okay, to let you in on the third of my favourite jokes from the 1960s. The story is a gentle one, as indeed, was most of the humour itself in those days. But, don't be misled, we as a group were right at the forefront, on the cutting edge, at the pointed end of the vanguard when it came to jokes and could appreciate the more satirical, aggressive and controversial of the country's comedians. We didn't, for example, flinch at the blue or sometimes crimson incisiveness of Ken Dodd.

We never closed our minds, or indeed, our ears to the humour noire of groundbreakers such as Ronnie Corbett or Arthur Askey. We even laughed heartily at the dark, satanic wit of Bruce Forsyth (Yes. Of course he was around in the sixties, and stretching the envelope or pushing the postcard, whatever the phrase is, too). So, having prepared you for the sheer bawdiness of it, here is my final and staggeringly apposite tale concerning the great movie legend, Cecil B de Mille. The B, though not as majestic as JMW Turner and not as downright odd as George 'Dubbya' Bush, stands for the equally inexplicable Blount.

Cecil B de Mille was a film director during the early days of cinema whose reputation as the master of the grand, epic movie was universal. In 1914 he founded Paramount Films with Sam Goldwyn but was best known for filming momentous and extravagant scenes involving vast numbers of people and animals in motion such as the Great War, stampedes of buffalo or bison or a horde of mounted redskin marauders. However, as often happens in such cases, it was said, and, incidentally, never denied by de Mille, that though the result of his own individual creativity and ambition, the success and the very greatness of these impressive scenes were almost totally due to the skill and experience of his cameraman and colleague of many years standing known to all simply as Joe. Joe had been at the top of his field for a number of years working almost exclusively for de Mille but respected and revered throughout the industry and beyond for his technique and dedication. He was, even in this the twilight of his career, a prodigious talent and only his employer and a few close friends recognised that his actions and reactions, both mental and physical, were not as sharp as they once had been and that his much envied powers of concentration were less sustainable than in the past.

So it was that shooting one of his last films, including the aforementioned redskin hordes, Joe was in position on a huge crane to shoot an overview of the whole scene from above. Another camera, let's say Camera One, was set up in a trench to shoot the horses as they leapt overhead. Camera Two was to take the scene from the rear and Camera Three from a little platform running along a track laid alongside the attacking host. At the early morning briefing it was made clear by the great man that, because of the massive organisation and expense involved, they had only the one chance to get the scene in the can but de Mille was confident that, with the resulting footage and quality editing, the effect would be staggeringly spectacular. The cameras were to film the whole of the action simultaneously and de Mille made it clear in no uncertain terms that filming must start the second he, himself, called 'Action'. This understood, the cameramen took up their positions, the horses became impatient, and the actors and stuntmen were tense with unconcealed anticipation. The moment arrived and the director bawled above the general furore 'one-two-three-ACTION'. The charge was on, horses were thundering, Indians were whooping, rifles were exploding, sweat was pouring, animals were tumbling, riders were thrown, arrows were shot in hales. What more could an audience want? The whole thing lasted just four minutes but it was surely the most realistic, the most authentic, the most terrifying charge ever caught on celluloid.

As was his habit the director did a quick check around. He pressed the button on his walkie-talkie and asked, "Okay, Camera One?"

Camera One replied, "I'm sorry, Mr de Mille, but a horse splattered mud into the lens after a few seconds. I got nothing, sir."

De Mille was fuming inwardly, but then hadn't he taken steps to cover just such an event.

"Okay, Camera Two?"

Camera Two came back sheepishly. "Sorry, Mr de Mille, an Indian crashed from his horse right before the event got underway and smashed the camera stand. I got nothing, sir."

Well at least he'd have some good action shots from the trench, he thought. He pressed the button again.

"Okay, Camera Three?"

"Sorry, sir, but the film broke after less than a minute. I got nothing."

De Mille was incensed. He'd spent all this time and money to finally cement his position as the king of epic movies and all these professional cinematographers had, on the day, proved less than up to the task. He was crestfallen, raging, almost suicidal when, in a flash, he suddenly remembered Joe. Okay he's getting on but he was still the best in the business. Elated and hopeful once more, his heart pounding, his mind racing, he pressed the walkie-talkie button again.

"Okay, Joe?"

Joe chewed on his gum, turned his cap round back to front on his head, put his eye to the camera and replied, "I'm ready when you are, Mr de Mille."

See. What did I say? I told you it was groundbreaking, fearless, on the edge and avant-garde. No, maybe on second thoughts I didn't. Never mind, it's still one of my favourites.

True to his word John coached and coaxed me throughout the whole tour with, I have to say, varying degrees of success. For instance in Tokyo's bullet train he somehow managed to fix it with the young girl wheeling the drinks trolley, who it should be said was, in Dave's words, 'the sort of girl who could make an old man very happy' (or should that be make a happy man very old?) either way she had agreed to slow down at a point where John lay prone in the aisle getting a terrifying realistic shot. As she slowed slightly he rolled clear of the trolley in the nick of time. Such professionalism. In my own attempt at the same shot

175

the trolley smacked straight into the lens of the howitzer almost taking out my right eye and two thirds of my nose. There you have a classic difference between an old hand and a novice. It appears it was a different girl on the trolley run and no one had thought to tell her of the intricacies of the whole artistic operation.

Similarly in the magnificent garden of Osaka, I took instruction in how to take a shot from behind one of the glorious cascades looking out through the waterfall. I'm certain that had I been a little more experienced I wouldn't have slipped and ended up filming koi carp in close-up. Luckily in three days the camera had dried out sufficiently for me to try my luck again. Emboldened by what I saw as a degree of prior success I set out unescorted to try to capture the essence of the chaos that was the rush hour of Tokyo simply so that I could show it to anyone back home with the temerity to moan about the relative peace and serenity that was the London traffic scene. Two very polite (I think) policemen escorted me off the central reservation and threatened to arrest me for 'bleaking the raws of load safety' and not taking the 'light plecautions'.

All in all, though, I felt that I came on in leaps and bounds, and at the end of the trip I couldn't wait to show my wife just how much I had achieved. We arranged to view the efforts of both John and myself at his home where he had a proper screen and all four of us were soon sat in rapt anticipation as he started his film. Right from the outset my heart sank when he screened a roaring lion (actually it was a kitten onto which he'd dubbed a lion's roar but, hey, still effective). He had subtitles, a commentary, background music, superb editing and, at the very end a charming little Japanese girl said 'Sayonara' and waved (even in the depths of humiliation I claim that as six languages).

It ran for fifty minutes or so and was, I have to say, superbly executed whereas mine was around eight minutes and in comparison of a slightly lesser standard. Who am I kidding? It was rubbish. I excused myself and went out to the car to fetch my filmic masterpiece. I opened the car door, took the film from my inside pocket and locked it in the glovebox.

"I'm sorry," I said re-entering the room. "It looks like we'll have to watch that again. I seem to have left mine at home."

(What's It All About) Alfie?

The title of this book may seem to have little or no connection, relevance or appropriateness for the actual content. In fact I have already assumed that most of those who have genuinely read this far in the book rather than having simply started wherever it happened to fall open can't even remember what the title is let alone how it could be in any way apposite. So, for those people and anybody else who is honestly interested in how these things work I shall try to untangle the web. (Why is it always a web that we have to untangle? Why not a mess, a network, a hotchpotch or simply a tangle?) I shall try my best to peel away the onion skins, break down the barriers, unfathom the plot that resulted in my finally settling on what, without the benefit of the arcane facts I am about to reveal, must seem to be a totally enigmatic, not to say wholly nonsensical, title.

It was in a slightly sleazy part of Wood Green that I spotted, in the window of a porn shop, the instrument that provided me with excitement, pleasure and satisfaction for the next thirty years of my life. (As I write this sentence my wife brings a cup of tea to my office, and glancing over my shoulder tells me I'd better rewrite this last couple of lines because of the awful mistake they include.) After a while studying in a frame of mind that could best be described as bemused and perplexed the penny, as they say, dropped and I rewrote the sentence thus.

It was in a slightly sleazy part of Wood Green that I spotted, in the window of a porn shop, the instrument that provided me with excitement, pleasure and satisfaction for the next twenty-nine years of my life.

Okay, I won't flog the joke any longer since it is clearly obvious to all of you, as it was to my wife, that I had employed the incorrect spelling of 'porn' and that what I really meant to write was in fact 'pawn'. As in pawn shops. Uncles. Three brass balls et al.

I liked to imagine at the time that the banjo, for that's what it was, had been the pride and the joy of an unsung virtuoso upon whose death his daughter was forced to hock it in order to buy shoes for her winsome, but, at the moment, barefoot gossoons. (I'm taking a bit of a flyer with this unlike 'caravanserai' earlier as I can't find it in my dictionary, but I'm fairly sure there's a Bing Crosby song including the line '...and see the barefoot gossoons at their play'. Mind you I'll look a bit of a munchkin if it turns out to be a puppy or some other creature.) NB: I've just remembered. The song is called *Galway Bay*.

That's what I imagined at the time and that I would carry on the tradition for years to come, although the truth was more likely to be that some snivelling little rat had burgled his next door neighbour's home and hocked the banjo to buy twenty weights and a bottle of Spanish fly.

The instrument cost me or rather my mother one pound three shillings and sixpence. The precise amount stays with me because some five years later that was exactly what my services were worth to Her Majesty's Government on a weekly basis. (No, not prison. National Service.) So, at the time of this seminal purchase I was thirteen and just two years into grammar school, sited with great serendipity just two or three doors away from Saville's record shop in Enfield Town. Each lunchtime or mid-morning if it were Wednesday and physics I'd stride impatiently down the road to check whether the record I'd ordered that month had arrived. If it had I would clasp it to my chest the whole of the thirty-minute bus ride home, rush straight to my bedroom, pull out our top of the range record player, (in truth a box with a carrying handle, and a turntable called a Dansettte) and lie on my bed eyes closed, a contented grin on my face and listen to the sensational singing and glorious song-writing of... Hank Williams.

Jazz hadn't come to me nor I to it at this stage. In fact that didn't happen for another year or so but the moment I heard Hank Williams sing his composition, *Cold, Cold Heart*, with the lyric, 'Why can't I free your doubtful mind and melt your cold, cold heart?', I knew my future was as a country and western singer-songwriter. The fact that I was thirteen, middle class and English was not going to stop me. No, sir, never.

What did stop me though, and bring this phase of my career to an abrupt end before ever it had begun was reading a book by another American singer, Burl Ives. (Hank Williams incidentally died after a brief life of booze and drugs and too much success in 1959. He was twenty-nine.) Burl Ives was a big, avuncular, bearded and extremely jolly man who sang songs like, *Foggy Foggy Dew* and *Big Rock Candy Mountain* and who, later in his life, starred in such Hollywood hits as *The Big Country* and Tennessee Williams' *Cat on a Hot Tim Roof*. His book, *Wayfarin' Stranger*, chronicled his journeys around America singing and collecting what was left of the country's folk music as had John Lomax and Carl Sandburg before him.

So, there you have it. I had the banjo, I'd read the book, any time now I'd be off. With my instrument strapped across my back I'd ride the freight trains along with the other hobos and at dusk we'd jump off at wherever the train had carried us. In no time at all one of the bums (I'm sure that's the right word) would manage to light a fire using his keen knowledge of the backwoods law and his Zippo lighter and we'd put a billycan full of sausages, a mess of beans and some wild groundhog nuggets to cook as we'd settle down to chaw baccy and spit in the fire till the grub was ready.

As we huddled nearer to the fire as some comfort against the near zero degree temperature, we'd tell each other that this was the life. Who needed a roof, a warm bed and clothes that weren't held together with dirt. We'd sing till we were hoarse then we'd chaw baccy and spit in the fire some more and say 'doggone it' every so often till it was time for chow. When we'd scoffed the wholesome but, nevertheless, revolting mess of groundhog nuggets and pork and beans we'd take a few swigs of something with all the tantalising nose and bewitching aroma of paint stripper. When we'd eaten and drunk our fill those that weren't violently sick would move a little further from the flames in case anyone should spontaneously combust. We'd say 'this is the life' a few more times, chaw some baccy and spit in the fire and then we'd settle down to get some sleep before the snow clouds burst overhead. Just before dawn I'd chaw some

179

farewell baccy, spit in what was left of the fire, bid a heartfelt farewell to those of my new-found but, it has to be said, evil-smelling 'compadres' and head out of camp. As I'd turn to wave a cheery 'adios' these happy, free-spirited gentlemen of the road would be busy burying the last of those who hadn't made it through the night. They'd spit in the fire and wave, muttering something scarcely discernable but sounding very much like, 'this is the life'.

With the joy and freedom of that encounter still occupying my every waking moment I'd set out to visit the foothills of the Appalachians to find and write down some of the glorious old ballads from the indigenous mountain folk whose hospitality was the stuff of legend. After scarcely three weeks journeying I'd come across a rude but totally uncomfortable-looking cabin in the middle of a forest clearing. On the veranda would sit a man and a woman both trying to light their pipes with a blazing clump of hay. The old man would rise and, dowsing the huge flames in his beard, he'd introduce himself saying, "Howdy there, young stranger, my name's Seth, why don't you set and rest a while? This here lovely lady's called Ruth. She's my wife... she's also my daughter... yeah, and she's the mother of my two lovely children."

With the introductions over the couple would take out their instruments and together we'd whoop and holler, yee haw and doe see doe for hours on end and all the time I'd stare spellbound at the unique way Ruth had cleverly adapted her fiddle style to get the best advantage from her six fingers (not including the thumb which wasn't best suited to fiddle playing due to its claw). As the sun peeped over the back of the cabin I'd start to strap my banjo on my back but Seth was having none of it, he'd tap the ground four times with his webbed foot and off we'd go again. Delirious with happiness and love for my fellow wayfarers I'd whisper to myself, "This is the life."

But, the way things do, just as I was about to book my passage, jazz happened.

I heard several recordings by Humphrey Lyttelton and his band and an American outfit called Lu Watters' Yerba Buena Jazz Band. Shortly afterwards with just a very brief time trying to absorb the music I agreed to do a gig (not a rowboat chiefly for racing or a light four-wheeled one-horse carriage but an engagement to play jazz etc) at Wood Green Jazz Club, where just a few weeks later I was to meet friend and inspiration, Lonnie Donegan. The job was with the Wood Green Stompers and we were to play support to The Saints Jazz Band from Manchester who were down for a couple of club dates and a recording session. Their own banjo player being unable to travel the band asked me if I would play the final set with them. It seemed they quite liked what they heard as they then invited me to play on the Parlophone recording session two days later.

I should say at this point that records in those backward, technophobic, wonderful days were issued as ten inch wax discs and those that survived for more than a few weeks were often heated up and moulded into plant holders. So, apart from the copies that I have any others still extant are probably holding a limp-looking busy lizzie or worse still a mother-in-law's tongue. Now, call me pernickety if you will but wasn't this section supposed to be about how the title for this book was arrived at? Yes, thank you. I thought so. The way this is going maybe we should have settled on *Six Musicians and a Borderline Amnesiac*.

Okay. We're back on track now. When traditional jazz started to take off in this country its basic instrumental line-up presented a challenge for, while there were bass players and drummers aplenty in the hundreds of dance bands large and small, pro and amateur across the country and young lads playing trumpets, trombones and clarinets in the likes of the Boy's Brigade, Salvation Army and the brass bands of the steel and mining towns still thriving in the North, where were the banjoists to be found? Apart from those doyens of the BBC's Light Programme and *Music While You Work*, *Troise and his Banjoliers* you could count the number of banjo players on the fingers of one hand. And that's a British hand, not an Appalachian one. So though the banjo is one of the easiest instruments to learn to play here lies the rub in this deliberation, it has to be said that it is unquestionably among the hardest to learn to play WELL.

So, you can see all those palm sweating, face erupting, trouser twitching adolescent males eager for the booze, girls and almost unlimited wealth that must be the ultimate destiny of all jazz musicians (all that is except for about ninety-nine percent) who had grabbed themselves a banjo, and after weeks of painstaking and painful effort had mastered three chords in three different keys, were either too idle, too unambitious or simply two sandwiches short of a picnic to acquire sufficient skill or knowledge to ever be anything more than mediocre musicians.

Now, do you see where this is going? As the other members of the band practised, rehearsed and progressed, most banjoists settled for 'just about enough'. You will, I sincerely hope, have noticed the term 'most of' in that last sentence because there were, and are still, a few exceptions and both I and they know who they are so there's nothing to gain by naming them. Although I will say at the risk of sounding self-congratulatory that I considered myself to have been better than average until, that is, one fateful day in 1963 when I was having coffee in the Star with a pretty good friend who occasionally wrote reviews for *The Melody Maker* or was it the *New Musical Express*. I can't remember. It may actually have been both but that point is of no importance to this story. At any rate he'd just been to review a new band in the New Orleans style and was preparing his review as we spoke. I asked out of curiosity what the instrumental line-up of this new group was, to which he replied, matter-of-factly, "Oh, you know, the usual, five musicians and a banjo player." Slightly taken aback, I said in response, "I hope you don't think of me like that."

My mind did a rapid summary of my defence should I need one to justify my exclusion. I played with currently the number one band in the UK; we'd had a single at number one in several countries. We'd played a *Royal Variety Show* and been on TV more often than the test card. Plus the legendary King of Jazz, Louis Armstrong, had been complimentary about us.

In case anybody should think that all that had simply proved was that I played with a good band, I had some months ago learned by heart a write-up by the great jazz pianist and veteran broadcaster, Steve Race, which read:

'Paddy is responsible for that blues-talking banjo in 'Saturday Night Function' and I recommend his solo to those anti trad folk who think that a banjoist's role is to go plink, plink, plink, plink, four times in every bar'.

At the time I thought about putting in on T-shirts but that seemed just ever so slightly over the top, not to say at some venues positively dangerous.

My companion spoke. "Don't be daft; I could never say that about you."

Great relief, and satisfaction, an ego remained undented.

He continued. "It's just not possible."

What a fine reviewer and jazz aficionado this man was. "No," he added. "You play in a seven-piece band, in your case it's 'Six Musicians and a Banjo Player'.

Well, that's it for now. I hope our paths cross again, till then remember:

Don't B$^\flat$, don't B$^\sharp$, just try to B$^\natural$.

CODA

It must be about three weeks ago now when a lady of a certain age, maybe sixty or sixty-five stopped me in Waitrose and said:

'Hallo. I know who you used to be. I used to follow the Kenny Ball Band in the early sixties. You were the banjo player, weren't you? I'd have recognised you anywhere. You haven't changed a bit.'

So, that's it in a nutshell. Rather than this ageless Pan-like, woodland deity strumming away gently on his lute I had, according to this good lady, looked, all those years ago, more like some grey-haired, old wrinkly ravaged by fifty or so years of sun, shiraz and cigar smoking.

Ah. Well. Maybe you'd be so kind as to pass me my rose-coloured glasses.